Raising Prayers, Not Hell

*Life Through the Eyes of
a Christian Teenager*

Brandon L. Boswell

Xulon Press
11350 Random Hills Road
Suite 800
Fairfax, VA 22030
(703) 279-6511
XulonPress.com

To my Heavenly Father, my family,
Cheryl, B.J., my church family,
Ashley, Shelley, and Carrie

Contents

Introduction vii

1 My Life in a Nutshell 1
2 Life Through the Eyes of a Teenager.................6
3 Family Vacations 10
4 Wisdom Teeth..15
5 Telemarketers and Televangelists..................19
6 My Favorite Salvation Experiences................21
7 High School...26
8 My Favorite High School Trip 32
9 My Most Memorable Christmas 35
10 Dating 40
11 Graduation 47
12 College Life 51
13 College Friends..56
14 What Makes a Good Baptist?.........................59
15 Baptists on Gilligan's Island 62
16 Preacher Murphy 64
17 Church Life...68
18 My Favorite Youth Group Experiences............74
19 Meeting Carman 78
20 The Mission Trip 82
21 Teaching Sunday School 89
22 Business Meetings..93
23 The Church Parking Lot 96
24 Vacation Bible School 98
25 The Worship Experience 101
26 Money Matters...104
27 The Scale 107
28 Hurricane Season..109

Conclusion 113

Introduction

When you hear the word 'teenager,' what is the first thing that comes to mind?

Do you have visions of long-haired, baggy-pants-wearing suspects being put into the back seat of a police car on an episode of "COPS?" Do you think of the people who work in fast food restaurants who ask you if you would like to order things off the menu you do not want or even know exist? Do you think of the people who drive around in multicolored, low-riding vehicles that make you wonder why on earth anyone would think a Honda Accord would look good painted like a bowl of fruit salad? This is certainly an interesting question to ask yourself.

Many people look at teenagers in many different ways, some good and some bad. So how should people look at teenagers?

A teenager can be defined as a young adult who is between the ages of thirteen and nineteen years old. Unfortunately, there are people who look at teenagers this way and only this way. There is more, however, to being a teenager than this definition implies.

This definition of a teenager does not include the thoughts, feelings, and emotions a teenager faces on a daily basis. This definition does not show how a teenager feels when the love of his life dumps him for someone who drives a nicer car, or any car, for that matter.

It does not indicate how a teenager feels when she is studying for a biology test which she feels could make the difference between passing high school and going to an Ivy League college or spending the rest of her life on a street corner giving quality windshield washing jobs to all the rich motorists who actually passed biology.

It does not describe how a teenager feels when he is studying for his driver's test for the umpteenth time because the last time he hit so many orange cones on the driving course you would have thought those cones owed him money or something.

The definition does not describe all the hard work a teenager must go through when he wants to buy his first car and he has to prove to his parents that in the long run the Porsche Boxster convertible will be far more economical than the Ford Escort. It also does not describe how a teenager feels when he is trying to work up the nerve to ask out the girl of his dreams when she doesn't know he's alive and would probably prefer to keep it that way.

Unfortunately, this definition of a teenager does not describe how a young teenager feels when she is pregnant and alone. It does not describe how a teenager feels when he is being put into the back seat of a police car because he thought that one beer would not affect his ability to drive. This definition of a teenager does not describe the feelings a teenager goes through when he finds out the girl he thought he'd be spending the rest of his life with doesn't even want to spend ten minutes with him.

As you can see, defining a 'teenager' as a young adult who is between the ages of thirteen and nineteen years old does not accurately describe everything you need to know about a teenager. As a teenager myself, I can relate to many of the problems encountered by this truly unique group. Fortunately, I have not experienced some of the more serious problems teenagers face.

At this point in my teenage life, I have discovered many things about life. There are two things I have discovered which many teenagers tend to forget.

I have discovered the importance of having a relationship with Jesus Christ in my heart and life, a fact many teenagers tend to forget. Many teenagers feel they are invincible and they think they can control their own lives. As a result of this thinking, many of these teenagers find themselves in situations they could have easily avoided if they had just let God have control of their lives.

I have also learned that many teenagers tend to forget the importance of having a sense of humor in their everyday lives. There are so many teenagers who take the tiniest things so seriously. They think that pimple on their nose will get so huge that eventually it will consume their whole face. They think that if that certain person does not go out with them they are destined to spend the rest of their lives living alone, eating unidentifiable things out of cans, and collecting cats as a hobby.

So many teenagers spend their lives worrying about the little things that will never happen. It is my personal belief that if teenagers would place their trust in God and develop a sense of humor about life, they could live much more enjoyable lives.

As you read this book, you will realize very quickly that I am a very ordinary teenager. The experiences I have gone through are quite ordinary situations that many teenagers go through. However, some situations are extraordinary.

As a teenager, I have learned to observe the situations I am faced with very carefully. I have learned that what seems unpleasant at the time can be used by God to help strengthen me spiritually and help me to grow into the kind of adult I know He wants me to be.

These stories and people are real. The names have been changed to protect the innocent. Actually, they were changed to protect me.

It is my sincere hope that as you read this book you will get something out of it other than a nasty paper cut or a splitting headache. So sit back, relax, and experience life through the eyes of a Christian teenager.

1

My Life in a Nutshell

I was born in the city of Jacksonville, North Carolina. I am a rare native of Onslow County. Very few people can say they are natives of Onslow County, and, unfortunately, very few people do say they are natives of Onslow County.

Jacksonville is a military community. We are the proud home of Camp Lejeune, Camp Johnson, Camp Geiger, and New River Air Station.

I'm proud to live in Jacksonville, but I must confess, with so many single marines stationed here, it's tough for a single civilian like me to get a date. It seems like every girl around here is either dating a marine or married to a marine. It must be the job women are attracted to, although I don't really know why.

Thanks to the strict military dress code, I have more hair on my head than most of the guys my age in my town have on their heads combined.

It is tough being a single civilian living in a military community. I try to compete with the marines in order to impress the girls, but it seems like the only way the girls are impressed is if you're trained to kill, jump out of helicopters, and run through the woods wearing camouflage trying your best to impersonate shrubbery. Personally, I feel that if I have to win a look-alike contest with a Carolina Pine in order to impress a girl, she probably isn't worth it.

Now that I've offended ninety percent of the people living in my town, let's move on.

I have lived in the same neighborhood all my life. It's a great neighborhood, but as time has gone by, the property values have gone down. Luckily, our neighbors have forgiven my family for that.

My family is a lot like other Southern families. We have cars parked on our front lawn as well as in the driveway, except ours still run. Not everybody in the South can say that.

God has given me many blessings over the course of my life, one of which is my family. My father is a retired college professor. He taught accounting for over thirty years. As you have probably guessed, he's quite the party animal.

He is also our church organist. He has been playing there for almost seventeen years. Many people might think it would be difficult for someone to find new music to play all those years, but not my father. He's been playing the same music for the past seventeen years and no one's even noticed. Every day he thanks God for the chance to work in a church filled with old people with hearing problems.

My father's hobbies include playing golf, checking bumper stickers for grammatical errors, and complaining to employees at fast food restaurants, but there's more to my father than that.

He also complains to cashier trainees and waitresses. No

one can ever accuse my father of being prejudiced. He'll complain to anybody, no matter what.

My father also makes a point of complaining about bad drivers. We've got many bad drivers in Jacksonville. Road work construction sites are just unofficial obstacle courses to drivers around here. If you ever move to Jacksonville and you want to invest your money in something, try a body shop. You'll clean up.

Here's a tip for anyone driving in a military community like mine. If you're driving a convertible and you get cut off by a convoy of military vehicles filled with armed military personnel, and you insist on yelling at them at the top of your lungs, make sure you are not riding with the top down.

My father also enjoys buying things, and when they don't work right, he likes to call up the manufacturer and complain until he gets the highest person in charge. We're all praying nothing ever goes wrong with his new George Foreman grill or else he might not come out of it alive.

My mother has a slightly different personality. She is an assistant elementary school teacher and has been so for the past fifteen years. She doesn't complain to cashiers, fast food employees, and bad drivers. She doesn't have to. Most of them are her former students and they're afraid to make her angry.

My mother is a very intelligent woman, but after spending so many years with little children, she has the tendency to think of me as an eight year old. To this day, I have never owned a pair of underwear that didn't have my initials written in them. I have also never seen what the crust on bread looks like because she cuts it off before I can see the sandwich.

It's not as bad as it sounds. I know someday I'll own initial-free underwear and eat bread crust. It's going to be a great day.

My mother can also come up with some of the strangest reasons for me not to do something. Just the other day, she caught me committing the unforgivable sin of scratching my nose with the tips of my glasses. She said, "Brandon, don't do that. You'll get nose dust on your glasses."

I've never heard of nose dust. Does it even exist? If it does exist, maybe the next time I come down with a head cold and can't breathe, I should spray my nose with Lemon Pledge if I want to clear my sinuses.

My mother also never forgets anything. If I do the least little thing wrong, she remembers it. I could be having trouble on an English term paper for a college course and the first thing out of my mom's mouth would be, "I hope we're not going to have another repeat of that D you got on that report on Arthur Ashe you did in the sixth grade."

Of course, life wouldn't be complete without at least one sibling. I have one sister named Patti. We have that typical brother and sister relationship. She thinks everything I do is the dumbest thing in the world and if I keep doing it, she is going to be so embarrassed she will have to change her name and go into hiding.

I mean it. I could be elected President of the United States, win the Nobel Peace Prize, and find the cure for every disease known to man, and the first thing out of her mouth would be, "Brandon, when the press interviews you, don't say anything that will embarrass me."

Patti is a pretty woman. She was even awarded the distinguished title of "Miss Onslow County." You can't get much more distinguished than that, although I had one friend who said the only reason she won was that she was the only contestant who could open a bottle with her teeth. That isn't true. At least four other contestants could. Don't you just love Southern humor? In another pageant, Patti was awarded Miss Congeniality. I still don't know how she managed to pull that one off, but she did, so I have to give her credit.

As you can see, I've got a pretty interesting family. We've had some good times and some bad times (I'll talk more about that later). Ultimately, no matter how bad things get, no matter how tight money is or no matter which family member passes away, we will always rely on the Lord to help us through it.

The memories I have of my family have also made me realize I need to make the most of my time with my parents while I still can. I have learned no one lives forever, no matter how much you want them to. I know at any moment my father could drop dead while he's complaining to the cashier at Wal-Mart or my mom could bleed to death as she is cutting the crust off my sandwiches. Lord willing, neither of these things will happen, but you never know. Once someone is gone, they can't come back. So if you're fighting with your parents or a sibling, make up with them. You never know when it's going to be too late.

I think my father's at the checkout lane at Wal-Mart as we speak.

2

Life Through the Eyes of a Teenager

Unfortunately, there are people who think teenagers don't have brains in their heads. This is far from the truth.

Teenagers are a lot smarter than people give them credit for. Teenagers can look at the world in a way that few adults would ever think about looking.

I'm no different. I wonder about many different things. I wonder about the television news. I wonder if some of these local television reporters actually listen to what they are saying.

Once during a local news broadcast, I heard an anchor person say, "Police officials are still searching for the missing guns. They fear they may have fallen into criminal hands."

I remember thinking, "That's a pretty good possibility. Either that or the Jehovah's Witnesses are tired of getting doors slammed in their faces, and now they're armed and they're not going to take it any more."

I also wonder about television commercials. I wonder if these people have any clue about what they are saying. Once I saw a commercial for a local mobile home dealer. The announcer said, "We offer special financing to all hurricane survivors." I remember thinking, "That's probably a pretty good idea, because it's probably tough for a dead person to be approved for special financing." I could be wrong, though. Since my grandmother's death, she's been approved for two different credit cards.

I wonder about the ads I see in the classified section of my local newspaper. I also wonder if the people who placed these ads knew what they were saying when they wrote them.

Once, I saw an ad for an Oldsmobile for sale. The ad said the car needed a hood, grill, radiator, and support. I'll say it needs support. That car needs so much support I'd think the owner needs to take it to a garage for a peer intervention group.

I saw another ad for a Cadillac that was for sale. The owner said he would sell the car for fifteen-hundred dollars firm or best offer.

Fifteen-hundred dollars firm or best offer? Which is it? I wanted to call the person who placed the ad and ask him what he was smoking at the time he placed it.

I wonder why every time I turn on the radio I tune in during a commercial that talks about the small amount of commercials on that station. I also wonder why God has given me the ability to stick my hand in a wad of chewing gum every time I put it down. I hate that. If I put my hand in a desk, I always end up putting it on a wad of old gum. When I put my hand on a counter, the same thing happens. I can be shaking hands with someone who is chewing gum and the gum will fly out of their mouth and land on my hand.

I wonder why so many religions make it so difficult to join their denomination. I'm a Baptist, and it's not like that in the Baptist church. If someone wants to join the Baptist church, all they have to do is walk down front and tell the minister they want to join. Then they are voted on, and if no one opposes them, they are taken to the fellowship hall to chow down on a casserole.

I also wonder about certain signs people put in their windows. Once, on a trip to St. Louis, I saw a sign in a window that read: "Catholic supplies coming soon." I remember thinking, "How come you don't see stores that cater especially to the needs of Baptists? I think there should be stores that sell only Baptist supplies. You can never have enough silverware and casserole dishes."

Probably the biggest thing I worry about is why am I so afraid to use any writing utensil other than a No. 2 pencil. This has always bothered me.

You remember what it was like. Your teacher would always tell you to use a No. 2 pencil to do anything that involved writing. My biggest fear was that I would be asked to write something and I wouldn't have a No. 2 pencil. Then I would have to spend the rest of my life in fear that they would find out I didn't use a No. 2 pencil and my diploma would be revoked. I knew I would have to miss out on a full scholarship to Harvard, a one-hundred-thousand-dollar-a-year job, and a new sports car all because I didn't use a No. 2 pencil on that geography test in the ninth grade.

This is a long-term fear. I'm still afraid that when I die and go to Heaven and they're checking for my name in the Book of Life, just as they're about to let me through the Pearly Gates, the Lord is going to find out that my name was not written with a No. 2 pencil and I'll be refused admittance.

Now that I'm taking a computer course, I'm afraid that they've taken all the names in the Book of Life and transferred them to a computer. With my luck, when I get to Heaven, they'll have lost my name in the computer, and as I'm being led away, all I'll be able to say is, "What kind of operation have you got going here? If this is supposed to be Heaven, why didn't you *save* the file on the disk?"

I'll admit some of the things teenagers wonder and worry about are a bit strange, but I can't think of a single adult who has never worried or wondered about something strange him/herself. The point I'm trying to make is that we all have our own unique way of looking at the world, and just because someone looks at it a bit differently than you doesn't make them wrong and doesn't make them any less important.

Teenagers need the love and support of adults in their lives. They need to know someone is out there who cares about what they have to say. If teenagers and adults would start listening to one another and sharing their ideas, who knows what could be accomplished for the Lord. So many people could come to know the Lord that on the Day of Judgment there wouldn't be enough time to see if every name was written with a No. 2 pencil.

3

Family Vacations

If you're a teenager like me, and you have parents like mine, sooner or later there will come a time in your life when you will have to endure that dreaded event known as the family vacation. I've had some of the worst family vacations known to man. They've been so bad that when I had to miss class to go out of town, my principal stopped asking for a note from my mother. He knew a copy of the police report would do just as well. Chevy Chase could do a movie on one of our family vacations.

My family has gone above and beyond what can be described as a bad family vacation. We've had the typical family problems, like the fact that my parents and I can never agree on which radio station to listen to. Most of the time we just ride in the car in silence for hours at a time. The only sound that can be heard comes from my mother's traditional three hour snoring marathon. The first fifteen minutes are kind of interesting, but after that, it gets pretty dull.

My father can snore even louder than my mother. Luckily, Mom always wakes him up before he drives into the guardrail.

Those are the typical family problems, but our problems go much deeper than that. Without a doubt, the worst family vacation we ever took was to Stone Mountain, Georgia. My sister had to be a bridesmaid in her friend's wedding, so the rest of us decided to go along and make it a little family vacation. Everything went well at the wedding, everything, that is, everything except for the horrible wedding cake they served at the reception. I know the bride and groom hadn't tasted this cake before the wedding because if they had, they probably would have taken it as a sign of things to come and called the whole service off.

After the wedding, we had the chance to do a little sightseeing, so we thought, all in all, we had had a pretty good little family vacation. We were never more wrong.

Now, my family and I don't really know what happened next, but this is what we think happened. We think the people of Stone Mountain, Georgia liked us so much that they all came together and tried to come up with a plan for us to stay a little longer.

They all came together and one person got up and said, "Hey, if we want to keep this nice family here, maybe we should offer them money." This idea, however, was voted down.

Then another person got up and said, "Hey, if we want this family to stay here, let's offer them food. After all, they are Baptists." This idea was also voted down.

Finally, a third person got up and said, "Hey, if we want to keep this family here, let's sneak onto their hotel parking lot, break their car window, hot wire their car, and take off." And sure enough, this idea was voted on and passed!

On Sunday morning, we went out to pack our car for the trip home. When all we could find were little piles of broken glass where our car had been parked, we knew we had been the victims of democracy in action. I can't describe how we felt as we looked at the empty parking space that day. We were all angry, shaken, and out for revenge. It was the same feeling you get when someone cuts in front of you in line at a church potluck dinner.

We walked back to the lobby of the hotel and reported the car stolen. The woman behind the counter said we would get a night's stay free because of what had happened.

As nice as that was for her to offer, it really didn't make up for losing our family vehicle, especially since my parents had to make only one more payment on the car. To this day, my father always makes sure everyone knows about that.

At that point, I realized that all those happy commercials I saw with happy families vacationing there are really unrealistic. We couldn't relate to those happy people.

Luckily, the parents of the bride whose wedding we went to were staying at the same hotel. We called them, and they immediately rushed down.

The mother of the bride ran up to my sister and me and put her arms around us and said, "Oh, I'm so sorry this has happened." Then to make us feel better, she said, "Please take some wedding cake." I was still trying to digest the cake I had eaten the afternoon before at the reception.

Then the bride's parents insisted on seeing the spot where the car had been stolen. They were absolutely fascinated by it. The way they looked at the spot, you would have thought one of the pieces of broken glass resembled a dead President or something.

Then came the fun part—watching my father call for a

rental car. He called one company and they made the unfortunate mistake of telling my father he had to order a car at least twenty-four hours in advance. My father said, "Well, if I had known the car was going to be stolen, I'd have called you twenty four hours ago!"

Finally, my dad located a car and the father of the bride drove him to the airport to pick up the rental. My mother, sister, and I stayed back at the hotel. My sister stayed in her room while my mother lay down in ours. I retreated to the bathroom and tried to plug up a leak with a piece of the wedding cake.

My father soon returned, and we packed up what belongings we had left and soon we were headed home. On the way back, we started making a list of all the things that had been stolen. To this day, I still regret the fact I didn't take any school work with me to work on, because I know I would have left it in the car.

To pass the time away, we counted all the out-of-state license plates we saw. No matter how hard we tried, we could never find ours.

Eight hours later, we were back home in North Carolina. We were all tired, cranky, and fearing for our lives, but we were home, and that was what was really important.

Eventually, our car was recovered, but the insurance company declared it a total loss. That's probably just as well. I was never going to get back in it anyway. I didn't know where the car had been or who had been in it. Once, I thought I saw our car being chased on an episode of "COPS," but I've never been able to prove it.

A couple of months later, my parents bought a new car. I learned shopping for a new car is fun. Any type of shopping where you get to sit down and ride around in a new vehicle to see if you like it is OK in my book.

Looking back, it was truly a memorable vacation. Even though we were robbed, God protected my family. Who knows what could have happened if we had gone out to pack that night. We could have been hurt, or worse. Remember, cars can be replaced. Your life can't.

This trip also taught me the importance of finding the humor in a bad situation. Anytime your family vacation pictures double as crime scene photos, you can't help but laugh.

4

Wisdom Teeth

If there is one thing teenagers and adults can agree on, it's that no one likes to be sick. I can't begin to tell you how much I hate being sick. I'll do anything to avoid contact with a germ. I can't stand touching doorknobs. When I'm on a date, I have the girl open the door for me. I know that isn't proper etiquette, but hey, I'm worth it.

I always overreact when I get sick. Every time I get a sore throat, I just know that in a matter of days I'm going to be knocking at Death's door. I just know my only hope for survival is Death mistaking me for a Jehovah's Witness and slamming the door in my face.

When it comes to being sick, I think there is a real double standard when it comes to men and women. If a woman sneezes, every man around her will be at her side in a matter of seconds with a box of tissues, a blanket, and a heating pad. If a man sneezes, every woman around him automatically thinks he's coming down with the first stages of the bubonic plague and must escape before it's too late. Luckily,

I've never been really sick, but I have had surgery. Recently, I had to have my wisdom teeth taken out, and boy, did I hate that.

The day before the surgery, I had to go to the dentist's office to watch a video on the whole procedure. After the voice on the tape explained the surgery, it went through a list of the possible risks. I didn't think the risks sounded all that threatening until the end of the list when the risk of death was mentioned.

So, right at this point, I was really psyched. I love the way they added death at the end of the list. It's like those car commercials you see on television. The voice on the commercial says you only have to pay sixty dollars a month for a new car, and just as you're about to rush out the door to buy that new car, they get to the end of the commercial and tell you that you have to pay so much money on the down payment that after you buy the new car, you'll have to live in it. You figure that since the offer is only good if you lease the car, you know you'll have to move out of the car in thirty-six months anyway, and then you'll be back to square one.

Finally, the day of the surgery arrived. I was really nervous, and after watching that inspiring video the day before, I was even more nervous. One moment I was sitting in the waiting room, reading a brand new picture Bible, checking out the "Girls of the Judean Countryside" photo spread, and the next moment they were calling me in for the surgery.

They put me in the dentist's chair, and the first thing they did was stick me with a needle. If there is one thing in this world I can't stand, it's a needle. The first time I got a flu shot, my mother said I could hold on to her, and by the time it was all over, she still hadn't regained consciousness.

As the surgery was about to get underway, the nurse tried to make small talk with me, which I figured was the least she could do after sticking me with a needle that could have been mistaken for a car antenna. Then she looked at my medical chart, saw my address, and told me that she lived only a couple of blocks from me. I thought, "Great! If something goes wrong, I won't have to walk very far when I hunt you down."

I really can't describe what I felt like while I was having my teeth yanked out of my head. The medicine they gave me through the needle made me relax and not think about it, yet I was totally aware of my surroundings. It was like I was asleep, awake, relaxed, and in pain all at the same time. It was sort of how I feel every time the sermon runs too long at church.

Finally, the surgery was completed. The nurse had to escort me to the car because every attempt to walk by myself made me look like someone you would see on those television police shows where someone has just flunked a breathalyzer test.

I felt sick to my stomach the whole way home. The only thing that kept me from throwing up was the fear that when my father bought the car he was too cheap to have the seats Scotchgarded and if I did throw up I would have to pay the cleaning bill.

I wanted to get home as quickly as possible, but it was like my dad was in no big hurry. No matter how hard I tried, I could not convince him to jump the curb and drive on the sidewalk.

I don't know why he didn't want to try. After all, we were in a four-wheel-drive vehicle. It's not like it wasn't capable of doing it.

Finally, we made it home, and I was able to puke to my heart's content. Because of the condition of my mouth, I had to eat soft foods for a week. I ate ice cream, yogurt, pudding, chili, meatloaf, fried chicken, and corn on the cob. Dad got a little carried away with the blender.

Luckily, my friends were extra nice to me after the surgery. I'll never forget the letter I received from my friend Jamie.

It said, "Dear Brandon, now that you've had your wisdom teeth taken out, does this mean you're stupid?"

Isn't it nice to have friends?

5

Telemarketers and Televangelists

I don't know why it is, but there has always been something about telemarketers and televangelists that bothers me. I'm not saying all telemarketers bother me, just the ones who have called my house. I had a telemarketer call me the other day. I can't remember what she was selling, but I didn't want it.

I said, "I'm sorry. I'm not interested."

I thought she would take the hint and hang up, but she didn't. Instead, she said, "Wait, I used to feel just like you before I heard about this product."

I thought, "Oh my gosh. This woman has been kidnaped and held against her will and forced to join an evil organized telemarketing cult where they have obviously brainwashed her. For all I knew, I could be her only contact to the outside world and it's up to me to save her." I still hung up on her, but I really felt bad about it.

Televangelists bother me, too. I'm not saying all televangelists bother me. Some of them I really like, such as Billy Graham, but others bother me.

Don't get me wrong. We need televangelists. They can reach many people. They go where people need to hear the Gospel the most, which causes me to wonder why I don't see more televangelists on the Fox Network.

Have you ever seen some of the sets from which these televangelists broadcast? My question is, if they are trying to convince people they are humble servants for the Lord, why do they have their sets decorated in a way that makes it look like they're broadcasting from the head office of the leader of a South American drug cartel?

I think that some televangelists are too commercial. One moment they're promoting the Gospel, and the next moment they're promoting a CD. When preachers are more concerned about selling tapes and T-shirts than they are about lost souls, they've lost out on the true meaning of worship.

Can you imagine sitting in church one Sunday morning, and your preacher says, "And if you don't turn and repent, you will spend all of eternity burning in the fires of Hell. Yes, the fires of Hell are hot, but not as hot as the prices at Mike's Auto World! Yes, if you don't turn and repent, you'll suffer for all eternity, but you'll never suffer at Mike's Auto World! In Hell, there will be weeping and wailing and gnashing of teeth, but at Mike's Auto World, there will be discounts on all late model Ford Escorts!"

Do you see what I mean?

6

My Favorite Salvation Experiences

When it comes to trusting Jesus Christ as your personal Lord and Savior, there are many people, especially teenagers, who feel the only way they can come to know the Lord is through some dramatic experience, like being involved in a major auto accident that results in a near death experience.

When I got saved, I didn't have that particular experience. That experience came later when I started riding with my minister. The way he drives, he could have an atheist singing the praises of the Lord by the time they reached the first stoplight.

I've had three salvation experiences. Three!

My first salvation experience occurred when I was in the fourth grade. I don't remember much about the fourth grade. All I really remember is that I had this dorky bowl-shaped haircut and I wore glasses. I looked like a nearsighted acorn.

I had been in Christian schools since I was four years old, but I had never thought much about salvation. However, this day was different. We had a Christian drama group come to school, and at the end of the service, they gave an invitation to anyone who wanted to get saved. I accepted the call and got saved that day, but I really didn't think much about it at the time. I was never baptized or anything.

About four years later, I was in the eighth grade at another Christian school. It was a Monday morning in February, and we had just started our annual school Spirit Week to celebrate basketball season.

You haven't experienced life until you have participated in a Spirit Week at a Baptist school. "Come Dressed as Your Favorite Casserole Dish" Day was especially enjoyable.

Anyway, it was a Monday morning and to kick off our Spirit Week we had a special missionary speaker who came to speak to us about the importance of salvation. At the time, I had been having some serious doubts about my original salvation experience, and this service seemed to make it worse.

As the missionary spoke, I realized I needed to get my heart right with the Lord. After the service, I decided I needed to talk to my principal, Mr. Strickland.

Later that morning I was in his office, and before I knew it, I was on my knees asking the Lord to save me.

It was truly the most humbling experience in my life, and it wasn't just because I got saved. It was because on that Monday it was "Kookie Kolour Klash Day" and I wasn't wearing anything that matched. Actually, now that I think about it, it was probably the best dressed I had ever been that entire school year.

Now you would probably think that this story would stop

here, but it doesn't. Several years later, I was on a week-long youth retreat in the North Carolina mountains. We had just had a very emotional service that night, and many people had made decisions for the Lord. Youth were crying. Chaperones were crying. I wasn't crying. It was like the service touched everyone but me and I wanted to know why.

By now, I was starting to get upset. Why were all these people affected by the service and not me? Why didn't I care? I mean, if anyone should have cared, it should have been me. I was a leader in my youth group. I served three terms on our youth council, the last term as president. I remember that because I was the first President of the Youth Council who was ever impeached, but that's another story.

After the service, we had our church group devotions. When it ended, I knew I needed to talk to one of our counselors.

I ended up talking to Dan. Dan was and still is a police officer in my hometown. He could snap your neck like a twig if he wanted to. Everyone knew that with Dan on the trip, if you got sent home early, you went home in a body bag.

Dan was also the kindest man you'd ever want to meet. I know it was God's will for Dan to be there that night.

After talking to him again, I found myself once again praying and asking the Lord to save me and forgive me of my sins. It was a very emotional experience, and I was a mess. That's why I'm sure God wanted Dan there because he is the captain of our city SWAT team and he has plenty of experience dealing with crazy people.

Luckily, I finally calmed down and Dan took off the hand cuffs and put away the pepper spray.

My third salvation experience was really awkward because I knew I needed to be baptized again, and I didn't know how the people of my church would react.

It turns out they were all excited about it. I soon realized I had been worried for nothing.

Finally, the Sunday I was supposed to be baptized came. I was really lucky because I was going to be baptized with a girl I had known for years. Well, we weren't actually baptized together. I mean, we're a friendly church, but not that friendly.

When I got baptized the first time, my minister forgot the words he wanted to say before he dunked me. I'm not sure, but I think the sounds of laughter from the congregation should not go along with the whole baptismal experience.

My second baptism was great, except for my fear of being submerged. In order to go through with it, I had to hold on to the side of the baptistry. If you could have seen the way Dr. Murphy had baptized the person before me, you would know that I wasn't trying to hold on to the old way of life, just life in general.

The biggest thing I learned from my multiple salvation experiences is that you should never be afraid to make sure you're saved. If you are having doubts, talk to someone who can help you. Do it while you still have time, because God never promises us tomorrow.

When it comes to salvation, all it takes is humility and prayer. You can't get to Heaven on good works or good looks. (That's a good thing, too, because if good looks were the only way to get to Heaven, I'd be trying to stay alive as long as possible.)

It's funny how people tend to forget these things. All it takes to know the Lord is believing Jesus Christ died for you and asking Him to forgive your sins and inviting Him into your heart and life. That's it.

Although if you get saved and plan to be baptized in my church, swimming lessons might be helpful.

7

High School

I'll never forget my four years of high school (no matter how hard I try). It's not that I don't have any good memories of high school, but it's just that the bad memories seem to overshadow them.

I went to a small Baptist high school. We had the strictest dress code in the world. In the four years I was there, the only leg I saw was a piece of chicken at a school dinner.

The thing I remember best about high school was my classmates. I'm sure they haven't forgotten me either, although I'm sure they have tried. Over the years, God has blessed me with many wonderful classmates who each have their own unique qualities.

First of all, there was my friend Rebecca. Rebecca never dated much in high school. Actually, I don't think she wanted to. One year during Career Day, she came dressed as a nun. When you come as a nun, that pretty much establishes the outcome of your dating life for the remainder of high school.

I had another classmate named Jamie (the guy who sent me the card after I had my wisdom teeth removed). You couldn't get much more Southern than this guy. I think his parents are to blame. On his first day of kindergarten, Jamie's dad packed him an RC Cola and a Moon Pie for lunch. I don't think he's been the same since.

Jamie was smart, though. When I was taking Spanish, Jamie always wanted to see my Spanish books. By the time I had graduated, Jamie had learned to say, "Hey, let's get in the truck and go hunting!" in Spanish.

Before my influence on Jamie, he was just an ordinary red neck. Now he's a bilingual red neck. Unfortunately, Jamie never achieved his goal of having the school song changed to "The Dukes of Hazzard" theme song, but we're all praying that someday his dream will come true.

One of my best friends was a guy named Alan. Alan was the most conservative person in the world. Back in high school, he was voted "most likely to form a militia." When the rest of the people in his senior class were checking out colleges, he was checking out compounds in Montana.

Jesse Helms once told him to lighten up.

My favorite story about Alan happened when he was involved in a little fender bender. He was driving with his slightly younger sister, Marie. Marie was never a very happy person. She was like a ray of sunshine to a sunburn victim. This girl could make a clown cry.

Anyway, Alan and Marie were rear ended. Shortly after this, a police officer was on the scene.

The officer walked up to Alan's car window, looked at Alan, and saw Marie next to him. He said to Alan, "Is she your girlfriend?" Alan looked at the officer and said, "Only in West Virginia."

Alan thought that was a pretty funny remark until the officer said, "Well, I'm from West Virginia." Luckily, the officer had a good sense of humor, and Alan should be eligible
for parole in about a year.

I think my best memories of high school centered around
my principal, Mr. Strickland. Mr. Strickland was great. He
was a military investigator back in the seventies. He loved to
tell us stories about his law enforcement experiences. His
stories would start out like, "My favorite arrest was . . . " or,
"The closest I ever came to shooting a man was. . ."

Many people might think these are not the kind of stories
that should be told in a Baptist school. All I know is that in
the four years I was in high school, we never had a single
detention.

Mr. Strickland was always concerned about my well
being. I remember one time my friends were teasing me
about my dating life, or more specifically, the lack thereof.

I told them, "I will not die alone!"

Mr. Strickland defended me by saying, "Don't worry,
Boswell, we'll make sure you have a dog!"

I knew he was just kidding. I never let the comment really
get to me. I mean, sure, I thought about jumping off a bridge
at first, but after a few months in therapy the suicidal ten-
dencies stopped just like that.

It's funny the things you remember about high school. I
remember how almost all of my teachers were related to one
another. I'm not kidding! My principal was also the football
coach, chapel speaker, bus driver, and my geography
teacher. His wife was my music teacher and the music director of our school plays. Their oldest daughter was our school
secretary, typing teacher, and algebra teacher. Her husband
was our Bible teacher and Spanish teacher. Their youngest

daughter was also a school secretary and her husband was the maintenance man. I was afraid that if I made one of them mad, I would make all of them mad, sort of like betraying a mafia family. I think every member of that family worked in the school. When my principal's oldest daughter gave birth to her son, we wondered if they would put him in charge of the kindergarten class right away, or wait until he got out of diapers.

I also have some bad memories of high school. One bad memory involved my high school administrator. I'll never forget the time he went on a discipline warpath. The administrator was Mr. Strickland's boss and we never saw much of him. In our school family, the administrator was like the weird uncle we kept locked in the attic whom we didn't talk about much.

On this day, however, he escaped. He said he wanted to speak to us. We thought he was going to talk to us about changing over to school uniforms the following year.

Man, were we wrong! Instead, his purpose in talking to us was so he could discipline people over petty dress code violations. By the time it was all over he had given five guys twenty-four hour dismissals because they had committed the unforgivable act of wearing their pants like shorts at a basketball tournament three months earlier. He also made them write five-hundred-word essays on rebellion.

I just sat there and watched the best looking, most popular, richest guys in the school reduced to nothing in front of their friends and girlfriends. Now that I think about it, it really isn't that bad a memory after all.

I also had more than one bad experience when it came to physical education. Sports was a big part of life at my high school, and I hated every minute of it.

Since my high school was so small, every guy was automatically a member of the football team. I think this was done to kill off the smaller and weaker guys so the star players couldn't help but look good for their girlfriends. I hated the way the girls looked at the football players. They treated them like they were God's gift to sports. They treated me like an athletic anti-Christ.

Another thing about high school that bothered me was the curriculum. Unlike public schools, we used a self-taught curriculum made up of little booklets called PACEs. When we completed twelve PACEs in a subject, we received a credit toward graduation.

What I really hated about PACEs were these annoying little stories that featured equally annoying cartoon characters. They were these annoying students who grew older as we did and they tried to teach us character traits as they lived their lives. This was a good idea except for one thing.

They were perfect. These teenagers never did anything wrong. I can't relate to that. Many times, we had to write the proper endings to stories in which the characters were involved. The purpose was to come up with endings in which everyone loved one another and there was peace and harmony in their perfect little, annoying cartoon land.

I hated doing this. These characters were so perfect they made me sick, but I always wrote proper endings because I didn't want to get into trouble. If I could have had my way, I would have had all the characters indicted on felony charges by the end of the first story. Yessir, nothing brings out peace and harmony like a car chase through three states.

One good thing about PACEs was the fact they were so light to carry. You could have five subjects that only weighed a pound. Unfortunately, I can't do that with my college textbooks. I'm lucky if my book bag weighs under fifteen pounds. Fortunately, I plan to take Legal Ethics next semester, so my textbooks will be a lot smaller.

I have many different memories of high school. Now that I'm in college, I can't believe it's all over. I've grown to miss my former classmates, and I'm sure in time, they'll grow to miss me.

8

My Favorite
High School Trip

My favorite high school memory was an overnight trip to a Baptist recreation camp at the end of my freshman year. We spent the whole night playing basketball, air hockey, and pool. We even went on a midnight boat ride on the nearby lake. Guys and girls weren't allowed to ride on the boat together, so we had to take turns with guy and girl groups. My principal said he made rules like this to prevent the guys and girls from getting too "close," but I think the real reason he did this was because he knew that if I rode with the girls, I would say something to them that would get me thrown into the lake.

I had gotten about forty-five minutes of sleep that night. When I woke up, my classmates tried to make me think I had missed breakfast. Here's a tip. Never make a Baptist think he's missed a meal. No good can possibly come from doing that. It has the same effect as riding around your town with a license plate that reads, "YOUR MAMA!"

Luckily, I hadn't missed breakfast and we were soon on our way home. On the way back, however, our bus started to have "mechanical problems."

Our bus driver, who was also the principal and the football coach, got out to check the engine. He came back in and said, "Now I don't want anybody to panic . . ."

How is it possible not to panic when someone says not to panic? He said, "Now I don't want anybody to panic, but we just had a fire on the bus. You need to get off the bus."

Picture this: a busload of tired, cranky Baptists, most of them having gotten less than an hour of sleep, who would bite off the head of anyone who talks to them because they are forced to sit on the side of a hot, dirty highway in rural North Carolina.

The conditions were just right for a business meeting.

I wasn't sure why the church bus caught on fire. All I knew was that if this was part of a judgment from God, I wanted to make sure the Lord knew I was not a member of that church and that the only reason I was there was for the free breakfast.

We made camp on the side of the road in front of an old house. To make the situation even more interesting, the old couple who owned the house drove up. They looked at us and said those words every person who's stranded on the side of the road wants to hear: "Has the man from the woods come out yet?"

I thought to myself, "No, he hasn't, but thanks for giving us something to look forward to." Luckily, another bus was sent for us and we were picked up before the man from the woods came out.

Nothing can spoil a trip like getting decapitated on the side of a road by a drug-crazed, chain-saw murderer, although I've heard that in some places in the South this is considered death by natural causes.

9

My Most Memorable Christmas

I love Christmas. I think it's the greatest holiday in the world, but just like anything else, there are some things I wish I could forget.

I'll never forget this one Christmas when I was a sopho-more in high school, and I had a school Christmas program, school Christmas banquet, and a church Christmas cantata all within a three-day period.

It all started during my school Christmas program. I had to go to a church Christmas party that night, so I was trying to get out of the program as quickly as possible. I had to play one of the three wise men, and naturally, with my luck, I was one of the last people to go on that night.

I arrived at the school and soon the program started. First, I had to endure a forty five minute piano recital. I've never liked piano recitals. I mean, the kids who are performing try their best, but let's face it, they have a knack for playing a song in the wrong key the entire time and not even knowing it. These kids had the ability to play any Christmas carol in a way that made you think it was the opening number of a horror film. I was fifteen before I realized "Silent Night" was not written by Stephen King.

After the recital, I had to endure a thirty-minute band concert. The band was so small you could detect every little mistake that was made.

Our band director was one of the stiffest people I ever knew, but she was devoted. Her baton was truly an extension of herself, which is good because it was the only way we could tell that she was alive.

Keep in mind that while all this was going on, I was trying to get out of there as quickly as possible. After the band concert was over, which if you had heard them that night, you would have thought it was over before it began, I finally got to do my part.

I tried to be a good wise man, but I just couldn't concentrate. While the rest of the wise men were presenting their gifts to baby Jesus, I was outside the stable checking my watch. I was looking at my watch so much I thought the principal was going to pull me off the stage and expel me because he thought I was trying to rewrite the Bible.

Luckily, he never did.

Finally, the program ended and I was soon on my way to the Christmas party. I think I was the last person to arrive, which was really embarrassing. I don't think it's possible for guys to arrive fashionably late. That must be a woman thing that God never intended for men to master because He knew if men ever did master it, they would never be on time for anything ever again.

This story doesn't stop here, however. The night after the

party, I went to my school Christmas banquet. I went alone that year. I hated going alone.

The girl I had asked to go with me had the nerve to turn me down, and to make matters worse, she turned me down at church. I couldn't believe she had turned me down at church. I realized this was one girl who was never meant to serve on a hospitality committee.

I'll never forget it. It was a Sunday morning, and I was getting ready to sing in the choir. I had asked the girl out on Thursday night, and I wanted to see if she had made up her mind.

Unfortunately, she *had* made up her mind.

I learned at that moment that finding out if a girl wants to go out with you is like being up to bat in a baseball game. I'll never forget the conversation. This is how it went and this is how I felt:

"Brandon, let's talk outside."

(Strike one.)

"Brandon, I really appreciate you asking me out . . ."

(Strike two.)

". . . and I think of you as a friend . . ."

(Strike three! Yoouu'rre out!)

Guys, I think you know that feeling pretty well.

I went to the banquet alone that year. I spent the whole evening talking to my friend's date. We really hit it off. The only thing that kept me from asking her out myself was the fact that my friend was a rather large individual who could kill me and, at that point in my life, I didn't want to be killed because I was still having some doubts about where I would spend all of eternity.

There's a picture of me in my high school yearbook at the banquet standing next to a cardboard cutout of a Salvation

Army Worker. The caption reads, "The Only Date Brandon Could Get."

I just know I left that high school warped, I just know it.

The night after the banquet, we had our church Christmas cantata. In keeping with my lucky streak, I had come down with a head cold and I was too sick to go.

I hated that! Our church Christmas cantatas are great. The choir dresses like angels and we have this massive set that is made to look like Heaven.

Of course, some of us didn't have the songs memorized, so we had to write the words down and hide them around the set. You would think we were in the bad part of Heaven because of all the graffiti we had on the Pearly Gates.

The only bad thing about our cantatas is this massive smoke machine they use when the choir comes out. I can't even describe the smell. If you stay in the smoke long enough, it's hazardous to your health. We're the only church in America who has had to issue a Surgeon General's Warning in the church bulletin.

Looking back on it, it was truly a memorable Christmas, but shouldn't all Christmases be memorable? So many people forget the true meaning of Christmas. They are so busy shopping and trying to find the perfect gift, they forget that God has already given us the perfect gift: His Son Jesus Christ.

What is even greater is that in order to receive this gift, we don't have to pay a thing. Jesus already paid the price for us on the cross so we could have the free gift of salvation, and it can be ours for the asking.

Kinda makes shopping for a new DVD player seem sort of dull now, doesn't it?

If you're wondering whatever happened between me and

the girl who turned me down, we've been able to put the past behind us.

But I still hope she doesn't need a character witness on Judgment Day.

10

Dating

I have decided to devote an entire section of this book to everything I know about women.

Now let's move on to the next chapter.

Just kidding.

Why do guys think they have to use pickup lines in order for a girl to go out with them? I never did that. I didn't have to. I went to a Baptist high school, and if a guy wanted a girl to go out with him, all he had to do was tell her God would punish her for all eternity if she didn't go out with him.

It was amazing how many girls I asked out who were opting for a warmer climate, if you get my drift.

I've always had trouble getting girls to like me. Once I was talking to a friend of mine named Mandy. I mentioned to her in casual conversation that I would not consider ever going out with anyone younger than a sophomore because I was a senior. Mandy said, "Brandon, I'm a sophomore. Could you say you wouldn't date anyone younger than a junior?"

I've learned some guys will do anything to impress a girl. I had a friend named Jesse who once named his gun after a girl. I don't know if that impressed her. I mean, if a girl named her gun after me, I would be impressed. I'd be afraid not to be.

I've never been what you can call a good-looking guy. I'll come right out and say it. I have the whitest, hairiest legs known to man. Back in high school, the other guys dubbed me the "Albino Ape."

My legs are so white that the last person who looked at them was temporarily blinded.

You get my point.

I also have a vision problem. I'm the most nearsighted person in the world. I was born wearing a pair of glasses, which supposedly made labor very difficult for my mom.

Because of my vision, I will probably never be able to drive. Therefore, I have to get people to drive me around. What is so great about this is that it gives me a chance to get rides from pretty girls.

When I'm in a car with a pretty girl, I always tell them that because of my eyesight, I have to get pretty girls like them to give me a ride. It's a great opening line.

I'm not sure what I hope will happen when I say this. All I know is that it hasn't happened yet, and for the sake of my testimony, it probably shouldn't happen.

I have never dated much. I've really only had a handful of dates, and the only way it can really be considered a handful is if I lose one of my fingers in a freak chain saw accident.

Actually, I have really had only one memorable date.

Her name was Emily. I remember many things about her. The first thing I remember about Emily was how quiet she was. She was a sweet girl, but I must confess, I've had more meaningful conversations with street mimes.

The second thing I remember about Emily was how modestly she dressed. I've never known a girl who covered herself like this girl. To this day, I still don't know what her knees look like. I'll never be able to prove it, but I think she came out of the womb fully clothed.

I remember one day I was staring at Emily and thought, "Man, she looks good in that bonnet."

The third thing I remember about Emily was she had the God-given ability to get upset about everything under the sun. I mean it! Everything that went the least little bit wrong would set her off. After she came out of the womb (fully clothed), the doctor slapped her on the butt and handed her a tissue.

I'll never forget the day I set Emily off. Neither will anyone else who was there.

Back in high school, we had to memorize Scripture verses every month and recite them from memory in front of a group for a speech grade. As luck would have it, Emily and I were in the same group. I was sitting with my friends and I wanted to show off for them.

Big mistake.

As Emily stood up to say her Scripture, I called out, "Go for it, baby!"

I thought it was funny. My friends thought it was funny. Heck, even the teacher thought it was funny.

Emily, however, did **not** think it was funny.

After I called her baby, she just stood there like a lump, a modestly dressed lump, but a lump none-the-less. Then she got this look on her face. I thought she was laughing. I had no way of knowing she was on the verge of an emotional breakdown.

Emily walked out of the room in tears. The rest of us just sat there in stunned silence. Then I finally came to my senses and realized I had to handle this situation in the most delicate manner of that of a God-fearing, Christian gentleman.

I had to prove none of it was actually my fault.

Now, after this, you would think I would not want to have any thing to do with Emily. After all, I called her "baby" and she broke into tears. If I had called her "honey," she probably would have jumped off the roof of the school.

Despite all this, however, I still wanted to ask her out.

I'll never forget the night I called her to ask her out. I hate using the telephone to call girls. If I'm going to get rejected, I'd rather they do it to my face. The only good thing about asking a girl out over the telephone is that if I make her mad, she can't slap me.

I called Emily on the phone. Knowing my past experiences with her, this was an extremely difficult call to make. I just knew I would say something that would set her off.

Every number I dialed was like loading a bullet into a gun, and putting the receiver to my ear was like getting ready to open fire. I just knew the moment she said "Hello" that my head would explode.

Still, I made the call, and she said, "Yes."

I couldn't believe it! No one else in the school could believe it either.

Our one and only date took place at our school's annual Christmas banquet. Our Christmas banquets were kind of like proms, except we didn't have dancing, skimpy dresses, and physical contact with members of the opposite sex. In fact, the theme for the banquet that year was "Six inches apart, please!"

I arrived at the banquet about fifteen minutes early and met Emily there. Her mom was a server that night and I suggested she ride with her. The reason I did this was that I was so afraid that if Emily rode with me something would happen to set her off. I was afraid that if we were stuck in traffic she would have a nervous breakdown. The way the traffic lights are in my town, anybody could have a nervous breakdown.

However, if something like that had happened, I think I could have handled it. All I would have to do was to jump out of the car at a red light. Since my parents would be driving, they could stay and comfort her. I could get away scot-free.

Yes, I am as sensitive as I sound.

Before the banquet started, Emily's mom took pictures of us. Emily had almost no expression on her face. She looked like the woman in that "American Gothic" painting. I felt like I should be holding a pitchfork and be standing in front of a farm house.

After the pictures were taken, we sat down to dinner.

Then it happened.

We found out some of the entertainment Emily and the rest of us were supposed to be doing that night had been canceled due to lack of preparation. Personally, I really didn't care. To look at Emily, however, you would have thought she had just lost out on the lead role in a Broadway musical.

I tried to calm her down and comfort her, but when you go to a school that prohibits physical contact with members of the opposite sex, there's only so much you can do. I couldn't hold her hand. I just sort of moved my hand around hers. My arm looked like a jumbo jet trying to get clearance to land on a foggy runway in the middle of the night.

It's probably just as well I couldn't hold Emily's hand. I don't know how she would have reacted to physical contact. For all I knew, her head could have started spinning around and she could have started to throw up pea soup, and since I had to help clean up that night, I didn't want the extra hassle.

Luckily, she settled down. My blood pressure soon followed. I thought it was all over.

But I was wrong. I was horribly wrong.

You see, Emily played the flute, and she was pretty good, but she wasn't classically trained, if you know what I mean. Emily had to play her flute that night for the part of entertainment that was not canceled. She got up on stage, and at that moment, I realized that if she hit one bad note on that flute, I was going to have to spend the rest of the evening feeling the wrath of "Hurricane Date."

As she started to play, I began to get really nervous. I felt like I was locked in a room with a ticking bomb. If I didn't try to diffuse it, I would be blown out of the building. If I did try to diffuse it, I would still be blown out of the building, and after my body was pulled from the debris, I would be expelled for violating the school's policy on physical contact.

Luckily, her piece ended and my peace began.

The banquet was soon over. It was getting late. It was going for 9:30 in the evening. For Baptists, that's late.

I told Emily I had a really good time, walked out of the building, got into my parent's car, and thanked the Lord for getting through the evening without the use of medication.

I really haven't had a date since then. I'm not sure if Emily has either.

I'm glad I asked Emily out for two reasons.

The first reason is that it filled up about four pages of this book just talking about it.

The second reason is that if I hadn't asked Emily out, I never would have known what it would have been like. Maybe things didn't turn out the way I wanted them to, but the Lord saw me through it.

Fortunately, Emily and I have remained friends, but we have gone our separate ways. She is away at college right now.

I think she is studying to be a grief counselor.

11

Graduation

After four years of high school, it was finally time for graduation. I had waited years for that night. I thought it would never get here, and neither did my parents, principal, and most of my classmates.

Unlike many graduating seniors, I got to know every member of my graduating class. It wasn't that I was a very popular person. It's that there were only four of us graduating. I knew I was going to take part in the shortest commencement exercise in the world.

My fellow seniors were truly memorable people. There was my friend Emily, you know, the "Crier."

Yeah, that one. I figured if I called her baby and she broke out in tears, it was going to take a team of crisis prevention counselors to get her through the graduation.

There was my friend Josh. Even though he's as American as they come, he thought it was cool to write things in Japanese. All the popular kids in my school thought this was cool.

I'm still trying to figure out what he wrote in my yearbook. The Japanese embassy has never returned my phone call.

Last, but not least, there was my friend Terri. My favorite memory of Terri occurred earlier that year on an overnight trip to a fine-arts competition in Winston Salem, North Carolina. We were staying in some cabins in the woods the night before the competition, and we were getting ready to roast some hotdogs over an open fire.

As we were walking up a hill to get to the campfire, I lost my balance and was about to fall. Just as I was about to fall flat on my face, Terri reached out her hand to grab me. Unfortunately, I grabbed her hand and threw her to the ground.

I stayed up, though.

Later, when we got to the campfire, Terri dropped her plate that held all the fixings for her hotdog. She said, "Oh, no, I dropped my buns!"

All I could think to say was, "Yeah, you've been doing a lot of that lately."

Luckily, she thought it was funny. If I had said that to Emily, I probably wouldn't be alive to talk about it, but luckily I was still alive and ready to share one of the biggest moments of my life with these truly memorable people.

Our graduation service was just like any typical graduation service, except it was much smaller. Also, because I was at a Baptist school, we had to decide whether or not we should pass the collection plate in the middle of the service.

We started graduation with the march down the aisle. Because I live in a military community, anything involving a march is taken very seriously. I still don't know if I marched down the aisle the right way. The thirty pounds of combat gear were pretty heavy and I kept losing my balance.

Then the point in the service came when each of us gave a little speech. This was a tradition in our school where the soon-to-be graduates had to say the nicest things possible about our teachers and principal without breaking out in uncontrollable laughter.

There are only so many nice things you can say about an algebra teacher who gives you an "F" on a test.

Finally, it was time to receive our diplomas. I was so afraid I would say or do something that would keep me from getting it, but luckily God gave me the strength to keep my mouth shut.

After the diplomas were handed out, which if I remember correctly took about forty-five seconds, my principal gave the commencement address. I can't remember a word of what he said. All I knew was I finally had my diploma. This was the night I never thought would come, and it finally had.

That night, I realized that all my hard work had paid off. There had been many times I wanted to give up, but I never did.

If I could offer any advice to any student, it would be to follow the teachings found in Philippians 3:14 (KJV) which states, "I press toward the mark for the prize of the high calling of God in Christ Jesus." This verse can be applied to all the areas of our lives, whether it be our relationship with God or our academic obligations. No matter what we want to do, we must work to make it come true. You can never accomplish your dreams by giving up when things get too tough. You'll never know what could have been.

Maybe you'll win and maybe you'll lose, but at least you'll know. If you lose, keep on trying. Remember, whatever doesn't kill you makes you stronger, or is it "whatever doesn't kill you gets you a movie contract and a book deal." It's one of the two.

The feeling I got as I held my diploma made all the hard work worth it. By the time it was all over, I was singing the praises of the Lord.

So was my principal.

12

College Life

After graduating from high school, I was happy to be moving on, and so were all the people who knew me.

I decided to go to a community college close to home. I still wish I had decided to go to a Baptist college. I knew no matter where I went to college, I would be suffering, so if I went to a Baptist college, at least I'd be suffering for the faith, but I had already made up my mind.

Going to a public college after spending so many years in a Baptist high school was quite a culture shock. I didn't know what my classmates were going to be like. For all I knew, I was going to need a police escort to take me to and from school every day.

It was weird going to a school that had security officers. We never had security officers back in high school. Of course, we didn't have crime, either.

Luckily, I slowly adapted to life at a public college, but I learned right away that it was going to take a while to adjust after spending so many years at a Baptist school. In one of my first English classes, my teacher held up the college handbook and said, "This is your Bible."

I thought, "Ma'am, I've read that Bible, seen its commandments, and frankly, I'm just not comfortable with that translation."

I'll never forget my drama class. I loved the teacher, but I hated the course because I had to hear some of the most ungodly scenes being read and acted out on stage.

After the students finished performing the scenes, the rest of us in the class had to tell them what we thought about their performance and what they could do to improve it.

I felt like I was sitting in the audience at a taping of Rikki Lake. I just knew that before this course was over, I was going to stand up during a scene and shout, "You go, girl! Tell it!" I guess that's how the cool people talk. I wouldn't know from personal experience.

I know college is supposed to prepare you for the future, but all this course prepared me for was to work security for the "Jerry Springer Show."

I also had to take a music appreciation course from a first-year teacher. She was pretty cool and she knew what she was talking about, but she had her faults.

Supposedly, she was a pretty good pianist, but we never found out because our classroom didn't have a piano. She always said if we had a piano she could play the pieces we were studying. After saying this for so many weeks, it got old fast.

By the end of the semester, I just knew she was going to say that if we had a piano she could play the piece we were studying and I was going to get out of my seat and shout, "Well, you don't have a piano, so just move on with your life!"

Luckily, I never did.

Sometimes she would forget what she taught us and assume we knew what we were doing. She would get pre-occupied with getting a music degree she was trying to earn from a state school here in North Carolina.

One day she told us she had to go up and explain her thesis to her adviser. She said she was asked a bunch of vague questions for which she really did not have the answers.

I said, "Now you know how we feel."

I probably shouldn't have said that, but the applause from the rest of the class made it all worthwhile.

I also had to take a biology course during the summer session. I'd like to stress the word "summer." It's my strong personal religious belief that summer school, Saturday school, and night school are all instruments of evil.

Fortunately, I really enjoyed my biology class. I learned some really cool stuff during the course. Our teacher told us about a guy named Gregor Mendel who spent his life cross-breeding plants to determine their genetic makeup. If there was ever a guy who needed a woman in his life, it was Mendel. I don't care if he was a monk.

Our teacher also taught us how to draw a genetic chart to determine what the offspring of their parents might look like. Someone asked her if there was any special way to draw the chart. She said, "No, but women are usually placed at the top and the men are placed at the side."

I'll let you write your own punch line to this story. I don't want to get slapped.

I also had to do a biology lab. Personally, I think giving me access to chemicals is a recipe for disaster. I knew in my heart that before it was all over, we were going to have a new skylight in the biology lab whether we wanted it or not.

I also knew I shouldn't get too attached to my mustache or eyebrows because I knew I probably wouldn't have them by the time the lab was over.

Luckily, I made it through the lab without the involvement of police and fire personnel.

Biology lab had its interesting moments. Once we did a mating exercise. (This story is a lot cleaner than it sounds, so please don't get my pastor involved.) In order to do this exercise, we had to pair up with other students and flip a coin to determine the genetic makeup of our children. We repeated this about four more times.

Kinda sounds like a game show on the Fox Network, doesn't it?

By the time it was all over, I walked out of the lab with a smile on my face and owing about fifty thousand dollars in back child support payments.

When I first started college, I thought my classmates were very intimidating, but the longer I stay, the more I'm getting used to them. I've really come a long way. I no longer run from class to class in fear of my life. I've started to make eye contact with the other students, and I've stopped watching "America's Most Wanted" to see what my classmates did over the weekend.

If that isn't improvement, I don't know what is.

Even though it's a lot tougher than high school, college does have its advantages. Since I went to a high school that had the strictest dress code in the world, it's nice going to a school where I can let my hair touch my ears and not be threatened with eternal damnation as a punishment.

It's also nice to know I don't have to dress up every day. I could go to class wearing shorts if I wanted to, and by golly, if my legs didn't frighten people, I would. I figure the less the girls know about me, the better my chances of getting a date.

College is tough and you need to study hard, but it doesn't have to control your life. If you plan your time wisely, you can succeed in college and still have time to spend with your friends.

Even I get to the beach occasionally. You can tell I'm there by the sound of girls screaming when they see me walking towards them in a pair of shorts.

13

College Friends

Soon after I started college, I got involved in a campus Bible study. There were usually only four or five of us attending, and most of us knew each other from high school. Normally, we would do a five minute devotional on the dangers of gossip and judging others, and then we would talk about all the stupid things our former classmates did that we would never do in a million years.

The friends in my Bible study are truly a unique group of people. One of my closest friends from the group is a girl named Allison. I went to high school with Allison and her twin sister, Sheila. Allison and Sheila had two of the cleanest records in high school primarily because when one of them did anything wrong, the rest of us couldn't figure out which one did it, so we never knew who to blame.

Allison was a unique individual. She knew I didn't have much of a dating life, so she would always tell me every intimate detail about hers to make me feel better, even though in reality, every story she told drove me one step closer to flinging my body off a bridge.

I'll never forget the time Allison told me about her first kiss. Normally, I don't like to hear girls telling how much they loved their first kiss unless I'm the one doing the kissing, and since I'm never the one doing the kissing, I've never enjoyed these stories.

Since Allison had been such a good friend to me, I decided it wouldn't kill me if I pretended to listen. Allison told me everything about her date that night. Personally, I really didn't care how many miles her date had on his truck when he drove her home, but she did.

Then she got ready to tell me about when her date walked her to the door. I was hoping the world would end before she got to this part, but unfortunately, it didn't.

Then Allison said, "Then he pulled me close and . . ."

I remember thinking that unless she tells me she pulled out a can of mace, I'm probably not going to enjoy hearing the end of this story.

Unfortunately, no mace was ever mentioned, and she still told me the end of the story.

Just as I thought the conversation was about to come to an end, Allison said, "Now, my next kiss occurred in October."

I think this girl had been keeping stats.

Another unique individual in my Bible study is my friend Gary. Gary is a naturally funny guy. Naturally funny people get on my nerves because I'm not naturally funny. It takes me hours of planning to be naturally funny.

During our school elections, Gary came into our Bible study and told us that for voting in the school elections, he was given a packet of Tylenol and hot sauce.

My question is, "How bad are the people running for student office that they have to pass out Tylenol just for voting.

And what was the hot sauce for, to wash down the Tylenol?"

Gary can really spoil my fun. One day during the Bible study, I was sharing with my classmates my belief that God was calling me into a ministry to witness to super models.

Hey, even the beautiful people need the Lord, too.

Gary said that particular job might be best suited for a woman. Jokingly, I said I'd be willing to wear a wig and a dress.

Then he said, "Well, then we would have to start a ministry for you because you'd be a cross-dresser."

I still think my ministry is a good one to pursue.

One of the favorite people in my Bible study was my friend Robert. Robert is the smartest guy I've ever known. I went to the same high school as Robert, and he was able to graduate a year early, and probably could have graduated three years early. No one could believe how smart Robert was. It was like his brain got bigger by the minute. During Bible study, when Robert would talk, the rest of us would sit and watch just to see if his forehead would expand.

No matter how busy I get at school, I always make sure I find time to spend with my friends at Bible study. The time I spend with them helps take the pressure off of studying for a little bit, and inspires me to study God's Word while in the company of fellow believers.

You never know what you can get from a Bible study. I've learned quite a bit during my Bible study sessions.

Above all, I've learned not to tell my friends my plan to serve as the chaplain on the set of "Baywatch."

14

What Makes a Good Baptist?

What makes a good Baptist?

As a Baptist, this is a question I often ask myself. To me, Baptists are known for two things: their love of food and their love of fighting. I've always wondered if the guy who invented the food fight was a Baptist who wanted the best of both worlds.

I don't think there has ever been a religious denomination more concerned about food than the Baptist denomination. Trust me, I know.

I went to a Baptist high school. Our school mascot was a roasted turkey.

Our senior trip was an overnight stay at the Waffle House.

I went to the only high school in America where my diploma was good for a dollar off my next purchase at Wendy's.

We thought the three parts of the Holy Trinity were the

appetizer, main course, and dessert. ·

It's just as bad at my Baptist church.

Next to my minister, the Wednesday night supper kitchen staff performs the most vital function in my church. They can cook a meal that makes you glad to live in the South. The other day, they cooked a Yankee pot roast and I was never more glad to live in the South in my life.

I'm just kidding. I have to make sure the kitchen staff knows that is a joke. Otherwise, they might quit and the rest of the church would come after me.

You should see a Baptist plan a lunch after an organized event. When a Baptist dies and the rest of his church is planning the funeral, they start with the lunch following the funeral and work their way backward.

It's like, "Ok, for the reception we're going to need two hams, one plate of deviled eggs, three casseroles, two plates of green beans, five cakes, two pies, and if we have time, let's make sure the deceased is buried in a coffin, so he doesn't spoil our appetites for the reception after the funeral."

Baptists are also known for their love of fighting. This is unfortunate, but if you've got good reflexes, you can learn to live with it.

A while back, my church was circulating a petition to have the "Jerry Springer Show" taken off the air. Personally, I think Jerry Springer would make a great Baptist.

Think about it. Everywhere he goes a fight breaks out. I mean, this is a guy who is destined to lead a business meeting in a Baptist church.

Can you imagine what life would be like if more Baptists were on television? Can you imagine what those reality-based video shows would be like?

We'd have shows called "When Baptists Attack!"

They could show videotaped footage of business meetings gone horribly wrong and show footage of fights that break out in the lines of potluck dinners because someone made the misfortunate mistake of cutting in line.

I know I'd watch.

15

Baptists on Gilligan's Island

Do you remember the show, "Gilligan's Island?" If you do, you will recall that on every episode the castaways always tried to find a way off the island.

I've always wondered what life on "Gilligan's Island" would have been like if all the castaways had been Baptists.

I think it would be something like this.

First, the castaways discuss building a boat to get off the island. They all think it's a good idea, but before they can get started, they have to have a business meeting in order to officially discuss the idea and vote on it, because as we all know, nothing can be done in the Baptist church unless it's voted on at a business meeting.

At the business meeting, they all decide building a boat is a great idea, but before they can get started building, they must appoint committees to look into the matter further.

First, the professor, who is the head of the handyman

committee, must find the cheapest way to build the boat in such a way that it doesn't force the rest of the castaways to swim for their lives in the middle of the Pacific.

The professor knows he has to stick to a certain budget because he has to present his supply list to the millionaire and his wife, who are the heads of the finance committee.

While all this is going on, the Skipper decides he should sail the boat. However, he can't sail the boat until the rest of the cast members vote on it at the <u>next</u> business meeting, so he gives his application to Maryann, who is in charge of the personnel committee. After she finds out how much the Skipper would charge to sail the boat, she must then get his budget approved by the millionaire and his wife on the finance committee.

After the Skipper's budget has been approved, the finance committee must go back to the professor's handyman committee and tell him they had to cut his budget in order to pay for the Skipper. At this point, morale is low and it looks like the boat building idea may not get passed, so in order to boost support for the idea, they turn to Ginger, the movie star, who is in charge of the publicity committee. Her job is to drum up support for the boat building idea.

Finally, the next business meeting rolls around. Before they vote on building the boat, however, Gilligan nominates Maryann to be a deacon. Since the millionaire and the Skipper can't comprehend the idea of having a woman deacon, they get upset and leave to start their own church on the other side of the island. Because of this, they don't have anybody to sail the boat, which is just as well because without the millionaire in the church, they would have lost all funding for the project, anyway.

Leave it to Gilligan to spoil another rescue.

16

Preacher Murphy

No matter how big your church is or how much money you have in your church budget, a church can never grow unless it has a good minister. I don't think any minister will ever be able to compare to my minister, Dr. Murphy.

Dr. Murphy has always been a firm believer in getting an education. He taught for thirty-two years at Baptist colleges in North Carolina. He even taught at one North Carolina college before it became a university.

I think this means that whenever Dr. Murphy finally left, the college could finally be upgraded to university status.

Over the course of his life, Dr. Murphy has worked in over forty different churches, but despite the fact he can't hold down a job, we hired him anyway.

Since I've spent a considerable amount of time with Dr. Murphy, I've started to notice some of the little things he does that make him unique.

One thing Dr. Murphy does is something called the invisible map. This is so cool. While he is talking about countries during Biblical times, he'll hold out his hand and just point where the country is located. It's like his hand represents the country or landmark he wants us to recognize.

I can really get into it. I've looked at his hand before and thought, "Is that the Red Sea or a mole or both? If it is both, maybe he can get it removed so he can show us the parting of the Red Sea."

I'm not sure Dr. Murphy knows where the countries really are himself, but since he uses the invisible map, we automatically assume he knows what he's doing, even if he doesn't. I admire him for that.

My favorite memories of Dr. Murphy involve going on Monday night visitation with him. Monday night visitation is our church outreach program where we go out on Monday nights to visit the people who came to the church service for the first time that Sunday. We try to encourage people to join our church and assure them that the sermons are usually much shorter than the one they heard that Sunday.

Many of the people we visit live in very exclusive neighborhoods. In order to live there, you must have at least three trucks on your front lawn, a satellite dish in the back, and own the biggest pit bull or German shepherd known to man. I'm terrified of dogs, so there have been times I didn't even get out of the car.

Despite all of this, Dr. Murphy has taught me the importance of being in the Lord's Army. Every time I see a pit bull staring at me licking its lips, I feel like telling Dr. Murphy that until we get out of this neighborhood, I'm working undercover in the Lord's Army.

Dr. Murphy has also taught me the importance of reaching out to those around me. Just the other night on visitation, we came up against a big dog. He said, "Brandon, reach out and see if it bites."

Dr. Murphy has also taught me the importance of walking in a close relationship with God. I taught him that the sidewalk wasn't meant to be used as a turning lane.

Dr. Murphy isn't the greatest driver in the world.

If you talk to him, you would know he can tell you how to get to Heaven. If you ride with Dr. Murphy, you would know he can take you there personally.

One week on visitation, Dr. Murphy met a police officer, a firefighter, and a paramedic.

The following week he met the judge, prosecutor, and the defense attorney.

Another problem Dr. Murphy has is his sense of direction. When it comes to finding a certain location, there are two things he likes to do.

The first thing he likes to do is to make me read street signs. Now, I'm the most nearsighted person in the world. Asking me to read a road sign is like asking Mr. Magoo to perform open heart surgery.

The second thing Dr. Murphy will do is drive very slowly and make me shine a flashlight on houses until he can read the right address.

We've met many police and security personnel this way. Yessir, nobody can dodge a bullet like Dr. Murphy.

Dr. Murphy is also a wise counselor. I've come to him many times for advice. He's very concerned about my future. The other day he asked me if I had ever considered studying abroad. I said, "I tried that one time and she wouldn't let me."

Another time Dr. Murphy told me he felt I should become an evangelist. I said, "At this point in my life, I'm more interested in partying, looking good, and dating as many girls as possible." He said, "Okay, how about a televange-list?"

(I'm only kidding about that, but if I ever do want to become a televangelist, I've got enough hair for it.)

The thing I admire most about Dr. Murphy is that he's genuine. He doesn't pretend to be someone he's not.

Sometimes I wonder about these ministers I see on television. These are some weird-looking people. You can never tell what their true intentions are because their hearts are hidden behind their hair.

Some of these people are large, too. They think practicing moderation is finding out how long they can stay at the buffet line in a restaurant without attracting the manager's attention.

I think some of these people know more about the second helping than they do the Second Coming.

Even though Dr. Murphy may not wear the fanciest suits or drive around in the nicest cars, he's always been there for me and the other people in our community, When it comes down to it, isn't that what being a minister is all about?

I'm sure Dr. Murphy will always be there for me in the future, and the way he drives, I'm sure it will never take him long to get there.

17

Church Life

By now, you might be wondering, "Brandon, is the rest of your church anything like your minister?" The answer to that question is, "Not really. Most of them know how to drive."

I've been at the same Baptist church in Jacksonville for almost my entire life, but I've only been a member for a little over five years. That was when the rest of the church knew they couldn't get rid of me, so they decided to let me join.

Just like Dr. Murphy, I've spent a great deal of time with my fellow church members, so I've started to notice their little faults, but despite this, many of them have had been big influences on my life.

One such influence is a Sunday School teacher named Tom. Tom has taught me about the value of a dollar. Many people think Tom is cheap, but he's not. Tom's just very careful with his money.

He still has the first dollar he ever made, and he says he'll let me see it the next time he opens his wallet.

That should happen in about three months. That's when we think he'll remember the combination.

Recently, I found out Tom's daughter is engaged. Everyone in the church can't wait to see how much Tom ends up paying for the wedding. We're all taking bets to see if, when it comes time to give her away at the wedding, he'll ask the groom for a receipt first.

I love to watch Tom using a cell phone. We'll be out on church visitation and he'll use a cell phone to call for directions. He loves doing this, especially when he uses my cell phone because he's too cheap to buy one of his own. To look at him, you'd think he was negotiating a multi-million dollar movie contract with Stephen Spielberg or something.

Another person who has had an influence on my life is a church member named Travis. Travis is a great guy, but he's more concerned about his hair than most women I know. He thinks putting on the armor of God means using the whole can of hair spray.

Travis is smart, though. He's taught me that God knows our needs even before we ask. I know this is true because God has always supplied Travis with the money he needs so he can keep buying the dye for his hair without having the bank foreclose on his house.

Many people might think being this vain would get Travis in trouble, but it has done just the opposite. It's helped him.

Recently our church was vandalized and two mirrors were broken. Tom said that since the person who broke the mirrors probably didn't like looking at themselves, we were able to rule out Travis as a suspect.

Travis is also the biggest flirt I've ever known, but despite this he knows a lot about women, and he is able to share his wisdom with the rest of the young men at church.

Before I started listening to Travis, girls would always ignore me. Now thanks to his advice, that doesn't happen anymore.

Now I get slapped by girls at least three times a week.

What can you expect from a guy who didn't want his son in the "True Love Waits" program because he felt there wasn't enough sex appeal?

Over the years, God has blessed me with many special friends at church.

One such person is my friend, Leslie. Leslie is one of the prettiest girls I have ever known, but she has proven every blonde joke to be accurate.

You could ask Leslie to define the three parts of the Holy Trinity and she'd say, "Lather, rinse, and repeat."

Once during Sunday School, our teacher told us that we live in the Milky Way Galaxy. Leslie asked, "What galaxy is Europe in?" Everyone in the church is hoping Leslie will marry well.

Leslie gets her personality from her mother, Debbie. Debbie is our choir dictator, uh, I mean choir director. I'm sorry, but I'm forever getting the two mixed up.

I'm not the only one.

Debbie is probably the most devoted music director we've ever had at church. She's so devoted she thinks the Great Commission is what she has to pay to people in order to recruit new choir members. This explains why she can't stick to her music budget.

Despite Debbie's faults, she has given me some great parts to play in our church musicals, despite the fact I'm just a lowly bass singer.

One year for a Christmas musical Debbie gave me my

most challenging role to play. I portrayed a tenor.

I knew that if I screwed up at being a tenor, she would arrange it so that the following year I'd be playing a soprano.

Debbie is also good when it comes to letting people use props. One year she let me use a loaded water gun. She even let me spray it out in the direction of the congregation.

I thought about shooting it at Travis's hair, but since I knew it was probably bolted on, I figured it was probably a lost cause.

When you stay in a church as long as I have, you also start to notice the little faults of your fellow church members.

I remember the time I was riding with a woman in my church named Belinda. When we arrived at our destination, I made the misfortunate mistake of shutting her car door in a decibel range that she could detect, so she said, "Brandon, don't slam the door."

I thought, "If you didn't want me to slam the door, why didn't you tell me not to before I got out of the car? Doesn't telling me not to slam the door after I've gotten out of the car sort of defeat the purpose?"

We have another church member named Penny. My favorite memory of Penny occurred during a progressive dinner at Christmas. (Oh, if you don't know what a progressive dinner is, it's when a group of church members gets into the ugliest church bus known to man and ride to different houses of other church members and eat a particular portion of a meal, such as an appetizer, main course, or dessert.)

Our church buses are so ugly that it's been rumored that when we drive one into a neighborhood, you can actually hear the property values drop.

Anyway, we drove to Penny's house for the dessert portion of the progressive dinner. We looked at the dessert table like the Israelites looked at the Promised Land.

We all knew Penny had gone to much trouble to prepare the food that night, so we were all gathered around the dessert table getting ready to take the food off Penny's hands and quite possibly the hands of the people around us who were holding the dessert we wanted.

We gathered around the table in a way that can only be described as swarming, and as soon as Penny came out, she looked at us and said, "In my house, I like to introduce guests to the table."

I looked at her and thought, "Ma'am, we've already introduced ourselves to the table, and you'll be glad to know, we really hit it off. In fact, if we were any closer, we'd be exchanging Christmas cards."

Luckily, she forgave us and we soon got our food. We had to push a few people out of the way in order to get what we wanted, but fortunately they fully recovered.

By far, one of my favorite church members is a fellow named Roger.

Roger's a deacon, but what is even better is that he's a semi-professional Elvis impersonator..

I think this is the coolest thing in the world. If you ask me, no matter how big a church is or how much money it has or how new their bus is, a church will never be what it could be unless it has at least one Elvis impersonator on the deacon board.

The only bad thing about Roger, our Elvis-impersonating deacon, is that he really can't sing. He just lip syncs to Elvis songs, but he does have the suit, though, and in the end, isn't that what's really important?

Roger's dream is to lip sync to an Elvis gospel CD during

a church service. (I'm not kidding.)

I think this is a great idea. I can just see it now. Our minister stands down front to give an altar call, while Roger stands up and lip syncs to "I'm just a Hunka, Hunka Burnin' Love."

Now that I think about it, maybe it isn't such a good idea.

As you can see, the people in my church are a unique bunch of people, and I think that is great. It's not fun being around boring people.

The thing that people tend to forget is that just because someone is different than they are, that doesn't make them boring. What we need to realize is that God makes everybody a little different, and He gave us all different talents and abilities so we could serve Him.

I think everyone needs to get involved in a church. You never know what you can get out of a church service until you go. If you're lucky, one of the deacons might do his rendition of "Heartbreak Hotel."

18

My Favorite Youth Group Experiences

I joined my church youth group when I was in the seventh grade, and I was a member for six years. I thought it was going to be seven. Luckily, my high school principal said I would graduate on time. Actually, he said I wouldn't be coming back the next year. I assumed that meant I was graduating. I was never sure, though.

In the six years I was in my youth group, we had more youth directors than I can remember. We went through youth directors like a televangelist goes through cans of hair spray.

One of my first youth directors was a woman named Dana. Dana had the looks of Shania Twain and the heart of Mother Theresa. We couldn't have asked for a nicer, prettier youth director. If you just looked at Dana, you received a blessing. She was with us for about two years, but unfortunately her husband received a military transfer like so many men in our town do, so she had to leave. We were all sorry to see Dana go, especially the male population at my church. I think some of the men in our church were thinking about kidnaping Dana before she moved so she couldn't leave, but they knew that if they were caught their wives would never bail them out of jail.

Dana was one of the most outgoing people I ever knew. She could always relate to youth on their level, but if someone crossed her, she would let that person know how she felt in the loudest and scariest way possible. Anyone who thought about getting on Dana's bad side had to make sure his/her health insurance was paid up because there might be a hospital stay in the immediate future.

After Dana left, a couple named Don and Kerry took over the group. They were great. Don was a news reporter for a local television station. He drove around in the news van from his station that had the logo and everything. It was the coolest vehicle.

Once when Don and Kerry were taking a girl and me out on a double date, they picked me up in the news van. I thought, "Man, this is so cool!" I couldn't think of a better vehicle to be seen in on a date. What was even better was that if I couldn't think of anything to say to my date in the van, we could just crank up the police scanner in the van and listen to that.

We had some great fellowships in my youth group. One of my favorite ones was our video scavenger hunt. We went around town and did stupid things while we were being filmed with a video camera. We did things like performing air raid drills in a parking lot and dancing in the middle of Taco Bell. To this day, I still thank the Lord our church van was able to outrun that police car.

Unfortunately, with every youth director we ever had, we always had to have fund raisers. No matter what we did or where we went, we had to raise money to do it. If you had to use the bathroom at church and you ran out of toilet paper, you had to have a bake sale before you could get any more.

We had some interesting fund raisers, some good and some bad. One of the worst fund raisers we ever did was when we tried to unload, uh, I mean "sell" these mugs that had a picture of our church on them. Originally, the youth group thought it was a great idea, but three years later when we were still trying to give away the mugs as door prizes, we realized maybe it wasn't such a good idea.

Another bad fund raiser we had was when we tried to sell "church discount cards." These were cards that had our church logo on the front and discounts to local businesses on the back.

It was supposed to be our biggest money maker ever. Of course, two years later when we were wallpapering our houses with the leftover cards, we realized that we were wrong once again.

Not all of our fund raisers forced my youth group to file for bankruptcy. Some turned out really well. One of the best ones we ever did was our annual "Rock-a-thon." Each member would get donations from people and sit in rocking chairs in the church fellowship hall and would rock for about twelve hours to earn the money we collected. I hope I didn't make you think we actually danced. After all, I'm a Baptist. We can't dance. I think it's written in the church covenant or something.

Only in my church could you earn fifteen hundred dollars just by sitting on your rear end and doing nothing for twelve hours. It's been said our "Rock-a-thons" have helped prepare some of our youth for careers in politics.

Another fund raiser that worked really well was our "Parents Night Out" fund raiser. This was where the parents in our church would drop off their demonic little angels and let the youth watch them for a few hours while they went out to eat, a movie, and therapy. I always managed to get out of these blessed events. Whenever one of these fund raisers rolled around, something would happen so that I had to miss it. I was never more thankful for a head cold in my life.

One of my favorite fund raisers was a car wash at my church. When I arrived at the church, I was told to go stand by a door on the other side of the church and yell if I saw anyone coming out the door. It turned out the reason they wanted me to do this was because someone had been living in the church and was spotted. They wanted us to make sure whoever it was didn't get out before the police arrived.

We're all for people making our church their church home, but we do have our limits.

Finally, the police arrived to search the church. Nothing starts off a car wash the right way like a little manhunt.

I loved my youth group, and I have a lot of wonderful memories. I've had many friends in my life, but the friends in my youth group are the ones who have stuck by me to this day.

I learned so much during my youth group days. Now, if I ever have to help head up another manhunt, I know I'll be ready.

19

Meeting Carman

I went on many trips with my youth group. By far, the most memorable one was an overnight trip we took to Carowinds in the Charlotte area.

Carowinds is great. It's an amusement park that was built on both sides of the borders of North and South Carolina, which means if I got a girl mad at me, she could chase me through two states instead of one.

On the day of the trip, our youth group left the church around four in the morning. This is how you can tell if you love your youth group. If you can get up at such an ungodly hour like four in the morning to spend a day with your group, that's love.

We rode for five hours and finally arrived at the park. I did what most people do at amusement parks. I complained about the weather, rode a roller coaster and tried to keep my lunch down, and bought an overpriced cap which I've only worn twice since I bought it, but this was not why I had come on this trip.

You see, the reason my youth group had gone to Carowinds was because it was a special Christian day there. For the entire day the park was to be the site for various Christian singers, and I'm not just talking about local groups. No, sir. They had the big names like 4 Him, East to West, and my personal favorite, Carman.

If you have never heard of Carman, you've missed out on a lot. Carman isn't just a contemporary Christian singer, he's **the** contemporary Christian singer. I think every song Carman has ever recorded has sold a million copies. Carman could sing a song about cleaning out his tour bus, and he'd win a Dove Award.

Carman was supposed to be the last performer of the evening, and he was the main reason I had gotten up at the ungodly hour of four in the morning and endured a day in a park filled with high prices, long lines, and crying children who had things coming out of their noses that even a coroner couldn't identify. Unfortunately, by the time we went to buy tickets for the Carman concert, they were all sold out: all thirteen thousand five hundred of them.

Needless to say this didn't sit very well with me. I couldn't believe it. Why did these things always happen to me? All I wanted to do was see Carman in concert, but I soon learned that God had a different plan for me.

By the time I had figured out a way to blame the whole day on my youth minister, it was time to leave for the hotel we were going to stay at that night before we went home in the morning. This is where the story gets interesting.

The directions to the hotel placed us in a residential neighborhood, which we all thought was strange. Then when we finally found the hotel, we discovered that it was located next to a thirty-story dilapidated building and an abandoned water park.

After seeing these things, we started to freak out. We wanted to know what kind of hotel our youth director had booked us in for that night. The only thing we were sure of was that with our luck, this was going to be our last night alive.

We were such a fun loving group. Can't you tell?

As we drove up to the front of the hotel, however, we realized we had the place all wrong. It turned out that our youth director had booked us in the old Jim Baker Heritage USA resort. Once we found out our hotel was founded by a televangelist, we weren't afraid of losing our lives, just our wallets. However, the best was yet to come.

Even though I was enjoying looking around this beautiful hotel, I was still disappointed that I didn't get to hear Carman. I know the Lord knew this because by his grace, I was about to get the biggest surprise of my life.

That night, I was in my hotel room. For whatever reason, I decided to go into the hallway. I don't know if it was the voice of God or a girl that called me out there. After all, I listen for both voices as equally as possible.

I walked into the hall, and I heard the words that gave me one of the greatest thrills of my life: "It's Carman!"

I couldn't believe it. Our youth group and Carman were staying in the same hotel! I knew right then it was the Lord who called me into the hall, and I'm glad I didn't put Him on hold.

Carman was getting ready to leave the hotel, and I knew if I wanted to see him, I would have to get to the elevator before the girls in my youth group went down to meet him. Fortunately, I'm used to running after girls, so I made it on time.

We finally arrived in the lobby and awaited Carman's elevator. I was so nervous. I was going to meet Carman, the greatest singer who ever lived. Then it happened.

The elevator came down, the doors opened, and there stood Carman! I was going to meet the man who was the contemporary Christian singer's answer to every question ever asked.

By the time it was all over, I had met Carman, gotten his autograph, and had my picture taken with him! I was so excited that one of the girls in my youth group told me to calm down.

That's excited.

All I had wanted to do that day was to see Carman, but instead I got to **meet** Carman. The only thing that would have made the day more complete was if he had offered to reimburse me for that overpriced cap I bought, but he never did.

I guess you can't win 'em all.

20

The Mission Trip

Over the years, I went on many trips with my youth group. The first trip I went on was to a youth conference down in Orlando, Florida.

To kick off the trip, we went to Disney World. I spent the day riding the fastest roller coasters I could find. I went up and down, side to side, right side up and upside down at fast speeds with my eyes closed and my mouth wide open. It's just like riding with my minister, just not as scary. My mother was a chaperone on the trip, and she didn't like the park much. She was never the same after "Space Mountain."

The great thing about this trip was that we stayed at the Hyatt Orlando. It was and still is the best place we've ever stayed.

The next year we went to a youth camp here in North Carolina. It was totally different than Florida. The camp was located next to a man-made lake. I know it had to be a man-made lake because God would never make anything that looked this bad.

Our living conditions were totally different from that of Orlando. The girls, of course, had a dorm that looked like the Hyatt Orlando. The guys stayed in cabins that bore a remarkable resemblance to the barracks on a rerun of "M.A.S.H."

What made the situation even worse was that the girls had air conditioning and the guys didn't. The first night we were there we were sweating like pigs and I had a first degree sunburn to make the situation all the more unbearable.

The following morning the guys and I were eating breakfast with the girls. I was hot, tired, and burnt to a crisp. As I was sitting there, one of the girls had the nerve to say in front of me, "I was freezing last night."

I can't remember what I was thinking at that time. All I know is I think I had to ask the Lord to forgive me for thinking it.

The next three summers our youth group went to a camp in the North Carolina mountains called Ridgecrest. We had some of the best experiences of our lives up there. They had the greatest cafeteria in the world. The preaching was good, too.

Can you tell I'm a Baptist who has his priorities straight?

After my third year at Ridgecrest, I was going to leave the youth group and move up to the singles class. Little did I know that my experiences on youth trips were not over yet.

The year after I left the youth group, I found myself on yet another trip with them. This time it was a mission trip to Nashville, Tennessee. I had never been on a mission trip in my life, so I knew this trip would prove to be one of the most interesting experiences of my life.

On the Friday we left for Nashville, I woke up around seven in the morning. We left that night shortly after nine in the evening, and I hadn't slept a bit since I had gotten up that morning.

I tried to sleep on the bus that night on our way up to Nashville, but I just couldn't. I can't sleep in a moving vehicle. I think this inability originated on my bus trips back in high school. I was always afraid that if I fell asleep on the bus, I would wake up to the sound of my classmates throwing me out of the emergency exit at forty miles an hour while my teachers and principal sat there laughing.

I wasn't exactly the most popular person in high school.

Now don't get me wrong. I tried to fall asleep on the way to Nashville. I tried counting sheep. I got up to fifty three, but I had to stop because the livestock truck turned off the interstate.

One of the other reasons I couldn't sleep was that our rented party bus had portable televisions in it and everyone was watching movies all night. If you've never watched the "Wizard of Oz" at one in the morning, you've missed out on life. Do you have any idea what it is like to be trying to fall asleep while above you hear the words, "Look, a twister, a twister!" or "Lions and tigers and bears, Oh my! Lions and tigers and bears!"

It's not as glamorous as it sounds.

After traveling all night, we finally arrived at the campus of Belmont University where we were to stay while we were in Nashville. By this time I had been awake for over thirty hours, so all I wanted to do was ditch the youth group and find a bed to collapse in for the next ten hours.

I wasn't that lucky.

Eventually, the camp staff came out and made us do jumping jacks while we stood in a straight line. I didn't want to do jumping jacks. I didn't want to stand in a straight line. Why do camp staffs put the campers through this kind of ordeal? Personally, I think it's because they don't get paid much, so to compensate for their salaries, they feel they are obligated to take out their frustrations on the campers.

By the time the worship service rolled around, I had been awake for about thirty-five hours. All I wanted to do was sleep, but once again the camp staff had other ideas.

When you go on trips like these, the staff really wants to get you involved in the services. They could get up there and shout, "Good morning!," and I would quietly say, "Hello."

Then they would say, "I can't hear you!"

All I wanted to say was, "Well, you should have listened the first time!"

Because we were on a missions trip, we were given the option of what kind of missions work we could do. I chose a creative ministry tract, which involved doing a variety of things over the course of the week.

One of the things I had to do was work with little children. Now, I don't have anything against little kids. It's just that I'm not very comfortable around them. Even when I was a little kid, I had to give myself a lot of space. It's not that I dislike little children, I've just never spent much time around them. After my parents had me, they decided not to have any more children.

Go figure.

I like little kids, though. They're like music to my ears, specifically, the theme music from "Jaws."

After the people in my group and I performed for the little kids, we had to play with them. It seemed like all these kids wanted me to give them horsey rides. They kept shouting, "Give me a ride! Give me a ride!"

Now, I can't drive, so I never thought I would hear anybody asking me for a ride, and now that it's all over, I pray nobody ever asks me for a ride again.

Little kids are interesting, though. I noticed little children have the unique, God-given ability to start crying for no apparent reason and stop crying for no apparent reason.

I thought only the girls I went out with in high school had that ability.

I had to work with kids on more than one occasion. In the middle of the week, we performed for a group of small children at a children's center in Nashville.

We put on skits and sang songs with the kids, and afterward we did face painting. Actually, I just stood there and watched the other people in my group do face painting with the kids. I didn't want to help the others because I just knew with my eyesight the way it is, if I started painting the kids' faces, it would only be a matter of time before I accidently gouged out some poor kid's eyeball with a Q-tip.

Before we left the center, all the people in my creative ministry group used the face paint to paint the first letter of our group on our arms. We thought this was a great idea until one of the women at the center said that in that neighborhood, writing symbols on arms was how the local gang members identified themselves.

I thought, "Well, this should be an interesting trip back to the church van."

You don't know how badly I wanted to jump out of the van and run around the neighborhood a couple of times with my "painted-on, Bible-study" gang symbol visible. Nothing wakes you up like taking your own life in your hands.

In addition to mission work, we also had fellowships at night. My favorite one was a parody of "Who Wants to be a Millionaire?" called "Who Wants to be a Missionary?" Instead of a million dollars, if you answered the million-point question correctly, you won an all expense paid trip to do missions work in London, England.

I was a contestant, and I *"wanted"* that trip. I was determined to see the sites of London even if I had to clean graffiti off of them.

We played the game just like the real show. Unfortunately, I was never picked to be on stage, and this really made me mad because I knew almost every question they were asking the people on stage. I couldn't believe they were asking such simple questions. I knew the answers.

I knew "Bug" was another name for a Volkswagen.

I knew "Magi" was another name for the wise men.

I knew "Sports Illustrated" was the magazine that had the swimsuit edition. For the sake of my testimony, I won't tell you how I knew that, just trust me on this.

I was really getting anxious to be on stage. By the time they were playing the third round, I just knew I was not in my right mind, but I was playing it cool so I wouldn't get the attention of one of our chaperones named Steve.

Steve was a psychiatrist, and he was as typical as they come. Steve was the kind of psychiatrist who could walk up to you in a cafeteria and say, "Excuse me, but I couldn't help but notice the way you peeled that banana. Do you have any unresolved issues with your mother?"

Yeah, that kind of psychiatrist.

I couldn't believe the way I was feeling about the contestants on stage. I was so concerned about winning that trip that all I could do was pray they didn't win. When we were backstage, we were shaking hands with one another. Now, I was planning the music for their funerals.

Luckily, God answered my prayer and nobody won the trip.

As I look back on my missions trip to Nashville, I realize I learned two very important things. The first thing I learned happened during that fellowship. I learned the importance of integrity in my life. I could be nice to the contestants if they lost out on the trip to England, but could I be nice to them if they had won the trip? I learned that when the chips were down, I let my emotions get the best of me. I remembered that God wants me to love everyone despite the situation.

The second thing I learned was the need to get out of my comfort zone. It's important to take chances and try new things once in a while. When it comes down to it, we all need to get out of our comfort zones. If Jesus Christ could die on a cross to forgive us of our sins, the least we can do is tell others about Him, even if it means leaving our neighborhood or town.

A week later, we arrived back home in Jacksonville. The weekend we got back, we made a presentation to the church that Sunday night about our mission experiences. We couldn't talk very long because we had a dessert fellowship after the service and some of the old people were starting to look like they were out for blood and a brownie at the same time.

It's very tempting to let that spirit of missions die over time after you are home. You get caught up in everyday life and forget about what you did for the Lord, but just because you're home doesn't mean you have to stop serving the Lord. You can serve the Lord no matter where you are. You need missionaries where you live just as much as any other community.

Besides, if you serve the Lord in your own community, you don't have to sit in a bus and listen to the "Wizard of Oz" at one in the morning.

21

Teaching
Sunday School

After six years in my youth group, I settled down for what I believed would be a long stay in the singles Sunday School class at my church. I knew I was going to be in the singles class for a long time because I had never had good luck dating. My last date had been with Emily, and I think we all remember how that one turned out.

With the luck I was having in my dating life, I knew that by the time I got a steady girlfriend, we would celebrate our first anniversary at my retirement party.

Things started out well in my singles class. Attendance was small, but we had a good teacher. Then, things changed. Our teacher left the church suddenly. I won't say why. She didn't do anything illegal or anything. I just want to keep you guessing.

Then it got interesting. My pastor had told me there was a chance I was going to be asked to teach the singles class.

I remember thinking, "Yeah, right. That will never happen."
It did.

On a warm November night, I received the telephone call from Sherry, our Sunday School Director. Now, at this point, I guess I should explain some things about life at my church. You see, in my church, Sunday School directors are like the "mob bosses" of the church family.

Now don't get me wrong. We've always loved our Sunday School directors, but with that love comes a deep-rooted fear of what could happen to us or our loved ones if we don't do what our Sunday School directors want us to do for them. The last person who didn't do what our Sunday School director wanted them to do ended up "swimming in the baptistry with cement shoes."

Just kidding, but it could happen.

Sherry really is a good Sunday School Director. She picked up where our last Sunday School director left off. Our old Sunday School director's motto was "See you in Sunday School." Sherry's motto is "See you in Sunday School, or else. . . "

Finally, my first day of teaching rolled around. I had two students. The first student came in and asked me where our old teacher was. I said I would tell her in a minute when the other students arrived. She said I would tell her now.

At that point I knew I had lost control of the class. I knew it would happen eventually, but I just didn't think it would be that soon.

Fortunately, as time went by, people realized there was nothing they could do to get rid of me, and things started getting better. Attendance went up and down, and so did my blood pressure, but I never gave up.

Believe me, some things really got to me. The first thing

that bothered me was that my students were getting married. Normally marriage is a good thing, but not when you teach a singles class and you're trying to keep attendance up. For every student who said "I do," that was one less student I had.

I tried to teach my students things that would help prepare them to grow as husbands and wives and more specifically as Baptists. I realized I had failed when I went to the wedding reception of two of my former students, Julie and Ron.

I realized that if I had done a better job of equipping them for a marriage within the Baptist faith, the newlyweds would have bypassed all that dancing nonsense and gone straight to cutting the wedding cake. I mean, these people were supposed to be devout Baptists. Where were their priorities?

I have lost three students to marriage. I always knew some people would go to great lengths to get out of my Sunday School class, but I never thought they would go that far.

Another thing that bothers me about teaching a Sunday School class is trying to get new supplies. It's like a life-or-death struggle just to get a book of stamps. I could write a made-for-television movie on the events that led up to my getting a new box of markers.

On the Sunday when I had my biggest class attendance ever, I told one of the members of the finance committee that I had broken my class record. He said, "Well, don't expect us to buy you a new one!"

Another thing that bothers me about teaching is when my students go away to college. My friend, Jenny, who was also my student, just recently left for college. Things like this concern me because I never know what kind of influences they are dealing with away at college. Many people can influence their thinking.

I asked her sister Julie, the so-called Baptist who would rather dance than eat cake, what Jenny would be studying in college. Julie said, "I can't remember what it's called, but it is the study of things that don't exist."

I know what it's called: My Love Life 101.

Despite all this, I've learned a lot from teaching Sunday School.

I've learned that the Beatitudes are not a singing group from Motown.

I've learned that suffering for the faith doesn't just mean listening to the head of our finance committee explain his top ten tips for avoiding a tax audit.

I've also learned "the peace that passeth understanding" goes a lot further than those extra twenty minutes of sleep I get every Wednesday night when our minister to senior adults says the prayer during our Bible study.

In spite of some of the down sides, I've never regretted teaching Sunday School. I don't know if I've helped any of my students make decisions for their lives, but I'm going to keep trying. Remember, you may never know what you've planted until it's a fully grown tree.

I know I'll always have problems with members of the finance committee, so I make an extra point to be nice to them. I have a great idea for a class project in December, and I don't want to do anything that would cause them to turn down my budget request for the mistletoe.

22

Business Meetings

By far, the most boring of church activities is that dreaded event known as the business meeting. We have the most boring business meetings in the world at my church. Our meetings could turn the most fun loving people into human tree stumps. If they started to record the business meetings at my church, we could sell the tapes to insomniacs and use the profits to buy a new church van.

We discuss many things at our business meetings. There was the time we discussed giving away some beach-front property that had been given to the church. Normally, we would never think of giving away beach-front property, but since the ocean had totally consumed the property at that point, we felt it was a lost cause. It's hard to enjoy an outdoor fellowship when you have to keep coming up for air because the finance committee was too cheap to fork over the funds for the diving equipment.

Our business meetings are so repetitious. First we have an opening prayer. Our deacon chairman prays God will guard our thoughts and tongues. Since Baptists are known for fighting, this prayer is said in order to prevent someone from throwing the first punch.

Then we recognize our church clerk to read the minutes of our last business meeting. She is so thorough with her notes, she could spend ten minutes reading the minutes from a six-minute meeting.

Next, we recognize our pastor so he can discuss upcoming church events. Following the pastor, we recognize the heads of our different committees to mention more upcoming events. Sometimes we recognize people we don't recognize.

Some people can sure ask some interesting questions at business meetings. At a recent business meeting, we voted on buying a new ice machine. Somebody actually asked this question: "What kind of ice will it be?"

I wanted to stand up and shout, "Frozen! What kind of ice do you want?"

My father said that it was a legitimate question to ask. I hope my life never gets to the point where I ask questions like that.

My favorite part of our business meetings is when they hand out our monthly financial report. To this day, no one has ever figured out how to read one of these things. We just sort of stare at it and nod our heads so that everybody else will think we know what we're looking at. We could be reading the sheet upside down, but we just don't know.

What's so weird about this is when someone works up the nerve to ask a question about the financial report, we look at them like they've just asked the dumbest question in the world. We look at them like, "How can anybody ask such a dumb question? Everybody knows the tax value of the choir robes during the fourth quarter."

It's my ultimate goal to find some loopholes in the financial report so we can come up with the money needed to buy a new church van. I'll look for any reason for the church to save money.

At our last business meeting, I looked at the list and thought, "Does our church daycare center *really* need electricity? I mean, the kids are there during the day when it's totally light out. We can open the doors and windows, let the light from outside in, and save two thousand bucks a month.

Business meetings may not be the most enjoyable church activity, but I think it's important for teenagers to get involved in church business. It's important for teenagers to know how their church is run.

You never know. Someday, the rest of the church might listen to my ideas. I might find the money for that new church van yet.

I still think we could save a ton of money if we canceled our minister's medical insurance. Anyone who can talk as long as he can on Sunday has got to be pretty healthy.

23

The Church Parking Lot

Whenever I step into my church, I am always filled with a renewed sense of joy and happiness. This joy stems primarily from the fact that once again I have made it through the church parking lot without getting run down in cold blood.

What is it about driving through a church parking lot that makes people want to recreate chase scenes from "The Dukes of Hazzard?" From the moment I step onto the church parking lot until the moment I'm in my car, it's a race against time.

I can't begin to tell you how many times I've come close to being sucked up the tail pipes of bitter old women in Buicks. Now, I'm not trying to single out old women in Buicks. Not at all. I've come close to being run down by just as many old women in Lincolns. I've learned you shouldn't expect much from church members who consider speed bumps to be personal challenges that need to be overcome.

I'll never forget the day my family became the victims of

another senseless church-parking-lot tragedy. I was showing some friends some damage to our family car from a hit-and-run accident the previous week. I swear my family was not the one doing the running. As I'm doing this, this little old lady in a big old Ford backs into our car in the exact same spot that had been hit the week before.

The woman stops and I say, "Ma'am, I think you hit our car."

That's when she took off.

I couldn't believe it! I had witnessed a hit and run in the church parking lot. Actually, it was more like a hit and crawl. I don't think she left the crime scene all that fast.

Later that week I told my friend Alan about the whole incident in the church parking lot. He said, "Why didn't you throw rocks at her car?" I don't talk to people much anymore.

I would never in a million years think of throwing rocks at a sweet little old lady, especially since that sweet little old lady could put her car in reverse and run me down flatter than a pancake at a Baptist Men's breakfast.

I would like to say to all of the people of my church and to all of the people who are reading this who attend church: "God has a plan for my life and the lives of other teenagers. That plan, however, is not to spend the rest of our lives as your hood ornaments."

Slow down!

24

Vacation Bible School

If there is one church activity I will always love, it has to be Vacation Bible School. I enjoy it so much because it's the only kind of school that doesn't assign any homework.

What's so great about Vacation Bible School is that it is for all ages. Years ago, our church advertised Vacation Bible School for ages "two to ninety-two." We thought this was a great slogan until a ninety-three year old woman sued the church for age discrimination. Luckily we settled out of court and changed the slogan.

We always do lots of cool stuff at Vacation Bible School. First, we come together for a big opening worship service. The highlight of this service is where we take up an offering for missionaries or various mission organizations.

The reason we enjoy this so much is that we always have a contest between the guys and the girls to see who can raise the most money. Of course, being the biggest cheapskate in the world, it's always a challenge to put money in the plate. Every time I do put money in the guys' bucket, the man holding it always gives me the same look.

I really don't know if it's a good look or a bad look. All I know is every time I put my money into the bucket, the man holding it gives me the same look. Either it's the kind of look that says, "Oh right, man, thanks for helping us out." Or it's the kind of look that says, "Boswell, you stupid cheapskate, is that all the money you're going to put in the bucket? I know you've got more money than that. As many times as the girls have turned you down for dates, not only can you afford to pay, you should want to."

You can say a lot in a look, can't you?

Our last Vacation Bible School was great. This year, I started going to the adult class, and I had my minister, Dr. Murphy, as a teacher. Since he has taught the Bible for so many years, he knows a lot of stuff, and he always wants people to learn more.

This year he asked us if we had ever played a certain game where you look up words in the dictionary and find synonyms to those words. I thought, "No, luckily I haven't reached that point of desperation in my life."

I think the most interesting thing about Vacation Bible School is the cool themes they have each year. Every year is a different theme and it gets better every year.

Recently, I was listening to our local Christian radio station and they had a guest on talking about Vacation Bible School themes based on a certain animated series that uses talking vegetables to teach the Bible. The person on this radio show was talking about having a Vacation Bible School based on these talking characters. She said the plan would start out with material for little children and move on to material for teens. Now, as much as I like the thought of these characters, I'm not so sure teenagers could relate to talking vegetables. Don't get me wrong. Teenagers express many vegetable-like qualities, but I think if a teenager is going to spend a week reading about the adventures of talking vegetables, whoever is planning this curriculum better make sure to come up with material to which teenagers can relate.

Maybe they could have themes like "Salad dressing that's too revealing," or "Tomatoes who develop an addiction to ketchup," or better yet, "Tomatoes with identity crises: I don't know if I'm a fruit or a vegetable."

I know I wouldn't be late if there were themes like that.

25

The Worship Experience

There are many different types of churches that worship the Lord in many different ways. In some churches, they feel the only way to get right with God is to get right with a rattlesnake first. In other churches, they feel that in order to experience true worship, you need to dance and shout and jump up and down.

I like these kinds of churches. You can worship the Lord and burn off those unwanted calories all at the same time. This is great. It's like the pastor is your own personal aerobics instructor. For every person who gets saved during the worship service, you can lose a pound doing all the celebrating. I think these churches should start videotaping their services. They could market the tapes as workout videos and make a bundle.

My church is slightly different. Even though we love the Lord as much as the people in other churches, we have always been more of a conservative church.

Don't get me wrong. If someone wants to lift his/her hands in our service, we don't have a problem with it. Since it doesn't happen very often, though, if someone did raise his/her hands, an usher would probably point him/her in the direction of the bathroom.

As much as I love worship services at my church, I've started to notice some weird things about them. For instance, I've noticed that our Sunday bulletin is treated like a sacred document and we think if we do anything in the service that is not listed on the bulletin, we could be doomed for all eternity. I mean it. If I came down with a cold during the middle of the week, I would have to call the church secretary and tell her I will probably need to blow my nose during the sermon so she can print that I will be doing this so that no one will be surprised.

I've also noticed that whenever anyone in my church sings a solo, everyone in the congregation turns into a judge on "Star Search." Doing a solo can make you or break you at my church. If you do a good job, you're on your way to becoming a famous featured unpaid soloist in the church. If you mess up, we'll give you that look that says, "You'll never sing in a worship service in this town again!"

If you can sing a solo in my church and not end up in therapy, you've got it made.

I've noticed how hard it can be to get people excited in church. I think the last time someone raised his hands in my church, he was choking on a piece of chicken at a potluck dinner in the fellowship hall.

I've also noticed how hard it is to get people to clap in my church. It's like they're afraid to. You should see us during an upbeat song. There will always be one person who is brave enough to start clapping, and before they even do that, I think they look around the sanctuary to see if anyone is carrying a concealed weapon. If they don't see that anyone is armed, they will make the brave attempt of clapping.

I've also noticed how people in my church act when the service runs too long. One time, we had a bluegrass group come to my church. The service was running long and I hadn't eaten in about eight hours.

In the Baptist faith, that's considered fasting.

At one point in the service, the group talked about the importance of "drawing nigh unto God." I thought, "I've been drawing nigh unto God for over an hour now, it's time to go home so I can start drawing nigh unto the refrigerator."

Luckily, God forgave me for that.

Even though there are some things about my church services I would change, we are always trying to make them better. We are clapping in church much more than we did before, and now people can raise their hands without the fear of being given the Heimlich maneuver.

Everybody has different ways of worshiping the Lord. The important thing is to find the way that is comfortable for you and that pleases the Lord. If you don't go to church, all you're doing is letting the devil get a foothold, and the longer you stay out, the bigger that foothold is going to get.

Try to get the most out of your church services, and if you haven't been going, go back. You never know what you can get out of it.

Just remember, if you ever sing a solo in my church and mess up, you may want to have someone waiting outside for you with the engine running.

26

Money Matters

I can honestly say without a shadow of a doubt I am the biggest cheapskate who ever lived. I'll do anything to save a buck.

My sister, Patti, you know, Miss Congeniality, has gotten on me in the past for being so cheap. She likes to shop and I don't, and she can't seem to understand how anybody wouldn't like to shop. In fact, she likes shopping so much, some of the local businesses in my town are thinking about having her gold card bronzed.

One day Patti said to me, "You're going to die a lonely old man who just sits at home counting his money!"

I said, "Well, at least I'll have money to count!"

My sister didn't like my saying that. My father was there too. He just laughed. I love my father very much.

If you're as cheap as I am, eventually everyone around you will start to notice. During church services, when they pass the collection plate, I break out in a sweat like an unbeliever sweats during an altar call.

I am convinced everyone who passes the collection plates in my church is out to get me. I don't know why they're so upset with me. It's not like I'm the first guy who ever put an IOU in the collection plate.

I don't know why they get so upset when I put foreign money in the collection plate. I say if you're going to collect money for the missionaries in Spain, what's wrong with putting Spanish money in the collection plate? They probably have to exchange the money to their currency, so this way I'm cutting out the middle man.

I really can't describe how the ushers look at me when I put money in the collection plate. They give me the look that says, "Oh boy, now we can buy those fuzzy dice for the church van we've been wanting for the past five years."

I'm also a cheapskate when it comes to dating. I don't know why so many guys want to date so young. My theory is, "why spend money on a girl you have almost no chance of marrying?" It is my strong, personal belief that Congress should pass a law that states if a guy is dating a girl and she dumps the guy, she should have to reimburse every red cent he spent on her.

By now, you can probably tell I don't date that often.

I challenge all guys everywhere who are reading this and agree with me to write their local Congressman to show favor for this law. Together, we can make it happen.

Fortunately, as I've gotten older, I have learned the importance of giving more freely.

Over the years, I've sat through my fair share of mission studies at church. I've seen videotape footage of missionaries and mission fields in America and beyond.

When I see the faces and the living conditions of the people on these tapes, it makes me think twice about complaining that I don't own the latest CD or own the latest gas guzzling, whopping eight-miles-to-the-gallon sport utility vehicle.

Maybe you don't live in the nicest house or apartment, or maybe you don't drive the newest car. At least you have a house and a car. The next time you complain about your roof leaking, remember that you have a roof. Not everyone can say that.

I've learned it's important to be a generous giver. It says in 2 Corinthians 9:7 (NIV), ". . . God loves a cheerful giver." It's also important to remember God owns everything. He just lets us use it, and He wants us to use it for Him.

So the next time the collection plate is being passed, give generously and cheerfully. You'll feel better about yourself, and the Lord will bless you for it.

What's even better is that you don't have to worry about the ushers following you home.

27

The Scale

Recently, my father purchased a brand-new bathroom scale. I hate scales. Baptists love to eat, so we believe any device that tells us how much we really weigh is an instrument of the devil.

Our scale is a bit weird. When we brought it home, I took off my shoes, and weighed myself in at about two hundred nine pounds. My father, also a devout Baptist, knew the stress that comes from weighing myself, so he did what any good Baptist father would do. He took me out for a burger and fries.

After we got back from lunch, I weighed myself again, but to my surprise, I weighed in about four pounds lighter. What was even more surprising was that after I rode our exercise bike for about half an hour, I weighed in eleven ounces heavier.

The following morning, I had two biscuits with eggs, bacon, and jelly. After that, I weighed in two pounds lighter!

This was great! It was like the more I ate, the more weight

I lost, and the more I exercised the more weight I gained. I realized this scale was obviously designed by a Baptist.

Wouldn't it be great if the more junk food we ate, the lighter we got? Unfortunately, it doesn't work that way.

This is also true when it comes to the things of the Lord. If you put the wrong things into your body, you'll be out of shape physically, and if you put the wrong things into your heart and mind, you'll be out of shape spiritually.

Physical exercise is important, but spiritual exercise is even more important. Just like you go to a gym to work out your body, you need to go to a church to work out your heart and mind.

Going to Sunday School and church are great ways to spiritually work out. Just think of your preacher and Sunday School teachers as your own personal spiritual fitness instructors.

Picking up your Bible can be just as effective as picking up weights, and a lot less stressful on your back.

So the next time you're in church, remember to get your spiritual workout, and remember not to cut in line during a fellowship supper. In the Baptist church, that's considered grounds for "justifiable homicide."

28

Hurricane Season

Having lived in North Carolina all my life, there are certain things I have come to realize.

I realize if I miss an episode of the Andy Griffith Show or Matlock, there will always be another episode after it, and if there happen to be any lost episodes, sooner or later, they will be found.

I realize that no matter who the President is, Jesse Helms will always be in charge.

I also realize that eventually I will be able to identify the brand of every cigarette made just by the smell. I think the only good thing about being around smokers is that they can't help but make my breath smell better than it actually is. Also, since smokers are taking ten years off their lives, they'll be less competition so I'll be able to flirt with more girls.

The biggest thing I realize about living in North Carolina is sooner or later it's time for hurricane season. We've been hit by so many hurricanes the past few years that the businesses on the beach could survive financially all year on the money the reporters from the Weather Channel spend alone.

When it comes to the Weather Channel, many people around here have become faithful viewers. I think that's because we've met all the reporters by now.

Last hurricane season, I saw an ad for a "Name the Storm" contest on television. I don't think this is a very good idea. Suppose you enter the contest and win. Let's also suppose the storm named after you comes and ravages your community. Once everyone in your town finds out the storm was named after you, you'd better pray the debris on the road has been picked up so you can get to the airport as quickly as possible.

If you were dating a girl and her house were destroyed by the storm named after you, it would take every box of chocolate and bouquet of flowers known to man to make it up to her.

Every time we're threatened by a hurricane, my family always does the same thing. First, we stock up on supplies. My father likes it when hurricanes threaten us, because it gives him a legitimate excuse to buy the canned meat and Vienna sausages he likes so much.

Then, when the storm gets closer, all the local schools close down, that is, except for mine. I always hated that. It seemed like all the public schools took a two hour weather delay every time there was a cloud in the sky. Once when a hurricane hit, I was in school just hours before it made landfall. While all my friends from public school were at home having the time of their life, I was at school trying to make it out to the car by using my book bag to keep my balance during the wind gusts.

After we're all home and safe, we sit back to watch news

reports of the storm all day. If the television reporters where you live are anything like mine, normally they're so happy and perky you'd think they were suffering from caffeine addiction, so it's a nice change of pace to see these usually perky and annoying people suffering from sleep deprivation because they've been up so long covering the storm.

Soon the storm hits, and my family and I sit in our house, and we watch the hundred-mile-an-hour wind gusts, and we always ask ourselves the same question: "Why didn't we park the car under the tree so we could collect on the insurance?"

We always forget because my father is always too busy loading up the cabinets with the potted meat and Vienna sausages to move the car.

After the storm hits, it's time for the cleanup process. I have the kind of neighbors who mow their lawns with sewing scissors, so it's a nice change of pace to see them pick a branch out of their yard. Of course, the trees on their cars is always a downside.

When our power finally comes back on, we always watch the footage of the storm damage. I have seen some of the most incredible and devastating footage where I live. It's amazing to see trees uprooted and whole buildings demolished by the wind.

With every storm, it seems I always ask the same question: "Why did God allow this to happen?" Truth be told, I've never been able to come up with an answer to that. All I know is God knows what He's doing even if we don't know what He's doing.

God never promised that storms wouldn't hit and houses wouldn't fall, but He does promise us protection. It says in Psalms 46 (NIV):

"God is our refuge and strength, an ever-present
help in trouble. Therefore we will not fear, though
the earth give way and the mountains fall into the
heart of the sea, though its waters roar and foam
and the mountains quake with their surging."

Nowhere in those verses does it say that bad things won't
come our way, but it does say that God is there to protect us
when the bad things come. The big question is, "Do we ask
God to help us only during the bad times and never during
the good times?"

The Lord wants us to rely on His help in the good times
as well as the bad times. Whether it be a hurricane, a major
exam, or a major date, the Lord wants us to rely on Him for
the strength and help we need to get through it.

I know that God will be with me through every hurricane.
I also know the potted meat and Vienna sausages will be
with me too. I think those things have a ten-year shelf life.

Conclusion

As I was writing this book, I really never wrote in any particular order. Whatever I had in my personal notes in front of me, I wrote down. However, this is truly the last thing I'm writing. As I'm writing this, the stupid computer is not lining these words up the way I want it to, so I'm not the happiest guy in the world right now. Sometimes when I read a book, I wonder what the writer was thinking when he wrote a certain section. Trust me, you don't want to know what I was thinking as I was trying to write these final words. It would kill all my credibility as a Christian.

Anyway, I've asked the Lord to forgive me, so now you can start to wonder what I'm thinking again. I have decided to close this book with two of my favorite verses, and as luck should have it, these two verses back up everything I've talked about in this book.

The verses are Matthew 6:33-34 (KJV). They read: "But seek ye first the kingdom of God, and his righteousness; and all these things shall be added unto you. Take therefore no thought for the morrow: for the morrow shall take thought for the things of itself. Sufficient unto the day is the evil thereof."

I think these two verses prove the two points I talked about at the beginning of the book—the need for trust in God and the need for a sense of humor.

None of us know what tomorrow holds and there isn't anything we can do about tomorrow until it comes, so why worry about it?

Throughout this book, I talked about the situations in my life where I had to rely on the Lord. Some were more serious than others, but they all called for reliance on God.

I also had to have a sense of humor during these situations. When your date starts crying or you get an "F" on an algebra test, contrary to what you might think, it isn't the end of the world. Just chalk it up to life experience and thank the Lord He gave you the ability to have that experience. Not everyone gets that chance.

I hope it has meant as much for you to read this book as it has for me to write it. It is my sincere hope that something I have said has touched your life in some way.

Remember, life is short, so make the most of it. You never know if that walk through your church parking lot could be your last.